How to Get Rich Slowly, But Almost Surely

How to Get Rich Slowly
But Almost Surely

Adventures in Applying the Decision Sciences

William T. Morris

Reston Publishing Company, Inc.
A Prentice-Hall Company

Reston, Virginia

© 1973 by
Reston Publishing Company, Inc.
A Prentice-Hall Company
P.O. Box 547
Reston, Virginia 22090

10 9 8 7 6 5 4 3 2

ISBN: 0–87909–343–9

Library of Congress Catalog Card Number: 73–76931
Printed in the United States of America.

Preface

There is a way to accumulate substantial amounts of money which is almost certain to succeed. It involves two notions which are both so obvious as to seem hardly worth mentioning, and so subtle that the vast majority of people completely fail to apply them. First, the way to get rich which has a very high probability of success is to do it slowly, deliberately, consistently, and methodically. Second, what it takes to do this is knowing very little about the stock market but a very great deal about yourself.

If this has the dull ring of nonsense, trivia, or very old stuff, hang in there a minute. What are your chances of getting rich doing what you're doing now? Give yourself a hard-nosed answer. Not very many people will get rich at all. What makes you different? Of those people and institutions which are wealthy, didn't the vast majority of them do it slowly, consistently, and methodically? How many people do you really know who got rich quickly and didn't end up poor again?

You're right to be very skeptical. This book tries to lay out a practical, no-nonsense plan of attack and give you the evidence that indicates it is almost sure to work. Almost sure to work, that is, IF YOU ARE WILLING TO CARRY OUT SOME EXPERIMENTS TO FIND OUT A FEW THINGS ABOUT YOURSELF.

In books like this, the author usually gives you the story of his astonishing rise to wealth and happiness and says you can do it, too. Since we are going to have some pretty tough things to say about such tales, I had better level with you right away. The ideas here are working for me. I have convinced myself of their validity over a period of twenty years of both being in the market and working at teaching and research

v

in Decision Analysis. Still, I hope you'll buy the book so I'll be a few pennies richer. My kids are almost ready to go to college.

We'll use the stock market as a working example, but all the evidence suggests that these ideas are used by people who get rich in real estate, bonds, or frozen hog bellies.

Contents

1

Making Your Own Test of the GRS Hypothesis

*The basic GRS hypothesis and why it's so powerful,
so obvious, but so seldom used to build wealth. Working out for yourself what you mean by "rich," getting
rich "slowly," and getting rich "almost surely." Why
it is essential to invest in a "get rich quick" experiment
in order to find out one of the most interesting things
you didn't know about yourself.*

Toughmindedness

Take a look at your own wealth of experience, your own common sense,
and try for a minute to separate what it tells you from the influence
of your emotions and your desires. The way to do this is to first try
to tell yourself what your emotions and desires are at the moment and
how they are likely to influence your thinking. Don't be too discouraged
if this seems difficult and unproductive at first. I'll have a good deal
more to say about this later. Take a hard-headed, tough-minded look
at the people and institutions around you and make a judgment about
the following hypotheses:

If someone had a reliable method of making fast profits in the market, why would he be so charitable as to let you in on it by writing a book or selling you an advisory service?

How many people can you actually identify who have made substantial quick profits in the market *and* been able to retain and enjoy a significant portion of their gains?

Of the very, very few people who do get rich quickly, does the visibility they achieve distort both their number and the ease with which it was done?

Considering the very large number of people who have devoted their energies to finding a system for "beating the market," what are the chances that one will ever be discovered?

You should get the idea that a hard-nosed analysis of your own experience is unlikely to encourage the notion that there is a high probability that you will get rich quickly. You might, but the chances seem pretty slim. Before you get discouraged, notice another significant piece of data. The vast majority of people don't get rich *at all*, let alone quickly. The idea that we will explore is simple enough. Your own experience, coupled with some fairly difficult exercises in self-control, will convince you that there is a fairly substantial probability of getting rich if you are willing to go about it slowly. This presents you with a tough basic choice:

To try getting rich quickly with a very small probability of success.

To try getting rich slowly with a very high probability of success.

To forget the whole thing and not get rich at all, as will be the case for most people.

This is indeed a difficult choice for most of us. It is far subtler than we usually suspect. To make the choice with any degree of reasonableness requires that we become a little clearer about getting rich, doing it slowly or quickly, and the ways in which one can operate so as to have a high or low probability of getting rich. The objective of this book is to help you work out these things for yourself, thus enabling you to make a reasonable and satisfying choice among the alternatives suggested.

The GRS Idea

Let's not waste your time by being deceptive about what I have in mind. If it is essential to get rich in the next few months, drop the book. We will be working with objectives that are 5, 10, 15, and 20 years in the future. If you are now twenty years old, we'll be talking about where you might be when you're forty. If you're now sixty, we'll be seeing what can be done by the time you reach sixty-five. Thus our planning horizons will be in years, not in weeks or months. You must also decide what you mean by "rich," but most of us are probably thinking about accumulating $10,000, $100,000, or perhaps $1,000,000. Just what you mean by "rich" is not an easy or arbitrary problem, and I'll have a good deal to say about how you might work this out. I will even say something about how important it is to try to get rich. Most people, as we look at their behavior, act as if they didn't think so. Finally, what do we mean by the chances of doing it quickly and the chances of doing it slowly? Again, you will need to think these propositions out for yourself, since it would have little effect on your behavior if you simply accepted someone else's views. Still, to give you something of a feel: I take the chances of getting rich quickly to be pretty small, less than 0.01 and perhaps less than 0.00001. These numbers, however, apply to me, not you. The chances of getting rich slowly, using the peculiar notions this book will help you develop, are pretty good, up around 0.80 or 0.90 and they get better as you progress. But these numbers must be developed by each of us for himself. The only purpose served by mentioning them is to help you decide whether you want to read on. It won't be just reading either. If anything is going to happen, you have to do some work, but perhaps not the kind of work you suspect.

The basic GRS hypothesis goes something like this: There is a very, very small chance of getting rich quickly, a very much larger chance of getting rich slowly, but most people will not get rich at all. I don't expect you to believe it, indeed I'd rather you didn't. What I hope is that you will get interested in testing it for yourself, since this is the only way it is likely to have any noticeable effect on your behavior. Only if you work it out for yourself will you actually do anything about it. You have to be really convinced of it, not just a willing skeptic. You have to stick with it, not just by making good resolutions, but by making it a natural, comfortable, self-consistent mode of decision.

The first thing to notice about the GRS hypothesis is that it proposes a trade-off between time and chances of success. Everybody would prefer "quickly" to "slowly" if the chances of success were the same, but the GRS hypothesis suggests that the chances are greater if you choose methods designed to do it slowly, far greater than if you try to do it quickly. To really understand all this, you must get used to the way scientists, engineers, mathematicians, and gamblers talk about risks or uncertainties. They talk about these dimensions explicitly, expressing their states of mind in terms of probabilities or chances. Making sense out of the GRS hypothesis, and making decisions which you will find generally satisfying, depends on developing this habit of being explicit about uncertainties.

Calculating Those Calculated Risks

Being explicit about our uncertainties is one of the real keys to reasonable, consistent financial planning and it is by no means as strange or difficult as it may seem at first. It is unusual, but growing less so all the time. If we are honest and tough-minded, we have to admit that we always have incomplete and imperfect knowledge of what the future holds. We can never be absolutely sure of what is in store for us. Yet, it is our unhappy practice in most decision making to suppress and perhaps ignore this uncertainty, often to our later severe sorrow. An event of seemingly modest import occurred a few years ago when weather forecasts began to appear with explicit expressions of uncertainty in the form of numerical probabilities for certain events. This may turn out to have been a matter of considerable consequence in our culture, for suddenly, all of us have to deal with and grow accustomed to these expressions of the incomplete knowledge of weather forecasts. It may mark the beginning of a general realization that these probabilities express the uncertainty in the minds of people in the National Weather Service, that they can be useful in making deliberate careful decisions, and that they can express all sorts of uncertainties that we must face.

The business of getting risks, probabilities, chances, odds, or likelihoods out on the table is so basic to our sensible participation in personal economic ventures that we should spend a little time on it right now.

To begin with, don't lose sight of what these expressions mean. They summarize your state of knowledge, your degree of certainty, your experience, your conviction, or your degree of belief in some statement. Don't get hung up on looking for the "right," or "correct," or "true" probabilities. These uncertainties are very personal. They say something about you, not about the stock market or any other external phenomenon. They may be based on data, past experience, expert advice, indeed, on all of our inputs weighed together.

Numbers like 0.50 or 0.95 are not essential. It is often extremely useful to express one's judgment by asserting that the probability of a certain stock going up is "high" or "very high" or "about the same as the probability of it going down." Numbers sound precise, but are often neither necessary nor accurate for the sorts of decisions we are trying to make.

Thinking somewhat vaguely about probabilities, chances, or odds is natural for most of us. Expressing these thoughts is less natural and thus more difficult, but essential. We need to get used to the idea of setting down measures of our uncertainty, to cultivate that habit, and make it a comfortable part of our decision-making style. This will take practice; practice which can be very profitably undertaken in all aspects of one's cognitive activity, not just in one's financial decision making.

Implementing a new habit involves considerable effort for many of us, but it is very likely that the effort will be well rewarded. It will make very difficult decisions much easier and more satisfying. It often reduces the worry and anxiety that accompany unexpressed uncertainties. It will help one make realistic evaluations of past decisions which produced good results as well as past decisions which produced not-so-good outcomes. It will help one be more reasonable in deciding what impact research findings, advice, or rumors ought to have on one's view of the future. It will help cope with the problem of whether to get more information before acting or whether to go ahead on the basis of what is already known. It helps one to see through (or at least into) such statements as: "The upside potential for this security is 10 points and the downside risk is 2 points."

Try writing down a few probabilities. Don't be afraid to; they can't be marked right or wrong. Based on what you know, what are the chances of a person such as yourself getting rich quickly? High? One in a million? 0.01? Very low? Now think about people who are already rich. What are the chances that they made it slowly and deliberately as opposed to quickly and sort of miraculously? You may find this tough, you may surprise yourself with what you put down, you may feel a strong need to get more data before putting down anything, but keep at it. Keep at it, that is, until you've made what you take to be an honest test of the value of being explicit about uncertainty. As we go on you will see how this tests fits into testing the GRS hypothesis for yourself.

A Little Practice

For openers, try being explicit about your uncertainty with respect to each of the 28 statements below. For each one, ask yourself about your degree of belief in its truth. What are the chances, probabilities, or odds that the statement is true? Before you start, set up three scales on which to express your state of mind:

Scale I: High   Moderate   Low

Scale II: Very High   High   Moderate   Low   Very Low

Scale III: 100   75   50   25   0

As you consider each statement, pick out a scale on which it is natural, comfortable, and reasonable for you to express your uncertainty. Some statements you may not understand, some statements you may simply have no "feel" for at all, but others may stimulate you to put a pencil mark immediately somewhere on Scale III. Keep track of your behavior in this little experiment and then ask yourself a few questions about yourself. Most of us find ourselves far and away the most fascinating subjects for experimental investigation. Data sheets appear on pages 117 and 118.

1/ San Francisco will play in the next World Series.

2/ A lot of product is known to be 12 percent defective. If two items are sampled from the lot, one will be good and one will be defective.

3/ I will receive a salary increase of at least three percent within the next twelve months.

4/ Our company's sales during the next calendar year will be greater than during the current calendar year.

5/ Ohio State will win more games than Michigan next season.

6/ If I were to throw an ordinary pair of dice, they would come up double threes.

7/ If I were to select a card at random from a well shuffled pack, it would be either an ace or a heart.

8/ The next time I travel from my home to work (school), it will take me longer than it did the last time.

9/ Over 95 percent of our customers are generally satisfied with what we do for them.

10/ A lot of product is known to be two percent defective. If two items are sampled from the lot, one will be good and one will be defective.

11/ The color of the mailman's underwear is green.

12/ A manned landing on Mars will be achieved by 1986.

13/ The prime rate will be higher six months from now than it is today.

14/ In five years fusion will be a larger energy source than will fission.

15/ All major types of cancer will be successfully treated within ten years.

16/ The next person to enter this room will be female.

17/ The median weight of persons in this room is more than 160 pounds.

18/ Since January 1, 1969, mutual funds have outperformed the Dow Jones Industrial Average.

19/ Housing stocks will perform better than airline stocks in the next twelve months.

20/ The Dow Jones Industrial Average will close up on the next business day following today.

21/ Jack Nicklaus will play in the next Master's Tournament.

22/ The winner of the 1966 NFL Championship was Green Bay.

23/ During the coming fiscal year our trade balance with West Germany will be in our favor.

24/ The next president of the United States will be a Democrat.

25/ At no time during the next two years will unemployment drop below four percent.

26/ The presidential nominee of the next Democratic Convention will be a governor.

27/ The senior Senator from this state is generally opposed to free trade legislation.

28/ If I flip an ordinary coin three times, it will come up heads twice and tails once.

Looking at all the statements, were you mostly unable to respond, or were you mostly able to give fast, easy responses on Scale III? This will tell you a little something about how well developed this mode of thought is for you.

Some of the statements deal with past events (Statements 11, 17, 18, 22, and 27) and some deal with future events (Statements 1, 4, 5, 8, and 12). Are there any differences in the ease or precision with which you express your uncertainty about these two types of events?

Similarly, we can categorize the statement roughly as to subject matter and ask if this reveals any interesting differences in the way we express our uncertainty (see Table 1–1).

Table 1-1

CATEGORY	STATEMENTS
Direct experience:	8, 11, 16
Cards, Dice, Coins:	6, 7, 28
Sports:	1, 5, 21
Stock market:	18, 19, 20
The Company:	3, 4, 9
Politics:	24, 26, 27
The economy:	13, 23, 25
Science & technology:	12, 14, 15
Sampling:	2, 10, 17

Are there differences when we compare those situations in which uncertainty expression tends to be socially acceptable (Statements 2, 6, 7, 10, 19, and 28) with those situations in which it is unusual and perhaps not quite so well accepted (Statements 3, 8, 11, 14, 16, and 22)?

What happens when we compare unique events (Statements 1, 5, 8, and 22) with events that can be repeated many times (Statements 2, 6, 7, and 28)? Does this indicate anything about the way we have grown up thinking about probabilities?

Still other little tests can help to develop self-awareness and show ways in which the useful habit of uncertainty expression might be encouraged. As you went through the series of statements, did anything happen along the way? Check what you did on the first eight statements with what you did on the last eight. On which statements did you most feel the need for more information? On which did you least feel this need? Which statements seemed easiest to answer and which most difficult? The point of all this, of course, is to get you to test the hypothesis that: You will find those decisions you make more reasonable, more satisfying, and easier to sleep with if you develop this way of thinking explicitly about uncertainty. Not only in your financial planning, but in deciding whether or not to carry the umbrella when there is a 30 percent chance of precipitation.

Risk Aversion

If you are willing now to talk about probabilities, we can try the GRS hypothesis in a somewhat different form. Suppose we agree that all financial opportunities will appear to us as having some degree of uncertainty about their futures. Suppose we consider a sort of principle of rational risk aversion which goes like this:

For a particular financial goal at a particular time in the future, what we seek are the financial opportunities which will maximize the probability of attainment (or minimize the probability of failing to achieve it).

There is nothing tricky about this principle of rational risk aversion. It is consistent with the way many of us would like to plan, it agrees with much of what we would do anyway, and it explains what a lot of people and institutions are trying to do. What is involved, however, is choosing a financial objective (How rich do you want to be?) and a point in the future or planning horizon. This is made difficult by the view taken by many people who have tried to look dispassionately at the financial opportunities which are available to us. We might almost dignify this common view by suggesting two very basic "laws" of economic life.

The first law of economic life:

The higher the financial objective we set, the lower the probability of obtaining it.

The second law of economic life:

The longer we have to attain a given financial objective, the greater the probability that we will succeed.

Again the trade-off problem, this time with two difficult choices. The richer we want to be, the smaller our chances of getting there. The more quickly we try to get rich, the smaller our chances of doing it. The rest of this book will help you to make your own peace with this troublesome, important, and most rewarding puzzle. To help in clarifying our notions of these uncertainties let's first look very quickly at some data. This data needs to be weighed with your own experience and your own particular skills and circumstances, not merely accepted.

I intend to argue a series of propositions which will seem obvious enough to many. Yet if they are obviously true then they imply a way of getting rich. In fact, most people who think my arguments are obvious will not get rich. This is still another instance of the crucial difference between the casual acceptance of an idea and believing it with sufficient conviction to act on it. These ideas are developed in detail because you must not just agree with them, but be willing to make the commitments which they suggest if you are actually going to get rich. We will look, for example, at the notion that there are relatively few rich people, not so much because this is a surprising feature of our economic system, but far more importantly, because we often act as if this were not true. To behave as if getting rich was easy is, to a degree, to act in a way inconsistent with the belief that there are few rich. If getting rich was easy, surely there would be many more rich people.

A Minute With the Income and Wealth Data

Our own reflections about wealth and our chances of having it are inevitably bound up with our notions about who is rich, how rich they are, and how they got that way. For most of us, the vague impressions we have gathered casually can be usefully checked against the small amount of data which is available. Getting such facts as we can about the wealthy tends to give a realistic perspective to our own calculations of objectives and probabilities.

However fascinating it might be to spend a few quiet hours talking to the computers of the Internal Revenue Service, we must be content with some severely depersonalized information. Looking at some people's adjusted gross income for 1971 is about the best we can do, although this leaves aside a lot of non-taxable dollars. See the table on page 116.

This data, like all of the data we will look at, needs to be interpreted by each of us, combined with our previous knowledge, and used to produce personal expressions of our own individual uncertainties. Perhaps, however, you will find some agreement with statements like: In terms of what millions and millions of people are telling the Feds, not very many have large incomes, they typically pay a very large portion of these incomes in taxes, and only a very, very few keep it all. Whatever the implications of this data for tax reformers, for most of us it means that the chances of finding one's self in a position of making and keeping a very large income are small. Very small indeed.

Looking at this same phenomenon from another viewpoint, it turns out that the top 10% of the people have 29% of all the income. The bottom half of all those who had income, had only 23% of all the income. The lowest 10% of those with income had only 1% of the income.

It is a little frustrating to wonder whether income produces wealth or wealth produces income, since both are true. If you have one, you are likely to have or to get the other. Wealth is still more unevenly distributed than income. Those who have been able to wring inferences from the very meager supply of data produce "gee whiz" statements such as the following:

The top 20 percent of the people have 56 percent of the wealth.

The bottom 10 percent have negative wealth—they owe more than they own.

The richest 20 percent have three times the wealth of the bottom 80 percent.

In terms of dollars, one way to number the rich is to note that in 1962, 4.1 million people (2.2 percent of the adult population) had gross assets of more than $60,000. Less than one percent of the adult population had gross assets of more than $100,000.

It's difficult to count the rich, and studies of this sort don't always agree, but that is not really the point for us. This kind of data says to me that the chances of having a substantial income are small and the chances of having substantial wealth are smaller. This seems to me to be a start at dispelling the notion that getting rich quick is easy or blessed with anything but a very, very low chance of success. It also suggests that if it is important to be wealthy, I'd better not just stand there. I probably should do something. Explore this kind of data for yourself and see what you think.

If it is difficult to count the rich, it is even more difficult to find out how they got that way. For Americans generally, about 5 percent attribute a substantial part of their wealth to inheritance. For rich Americans, getting it from one's ancestors is far more often the way. Of those who have at least $500,000, 34 percent attribute a substantial portion to inheritance, and this rises to 57 percent of those who have wealth of more than $100,000. Beyond this, there really isn't much data as to how they did it, and we must fall back on judgments based on our own experience.

How the rich hold their riches is probably some remote clue as to how some of them got that way. In 1962, 1 percent of all the wealth holders held 62 percent of all stocks which were publicly held. The richest 20 percent held an astonishing 97 percent of all publicly held stock. The top wealth holders had 43 percent of their assets in stock and 25 percent in real estate. These studies may or may not be showing us something about how they accumulated their riches.

Once again, each of us must interpret this kind of data with his own background of experience and expectations for the future. Maybe all the really rich people you know have ancestors who were bootleggers. Maybe Uncle Charlie is loaded and seems likely to return your kindnesses in his will. Perhaps, on the other hand, you will find that to some degree you can accept inferences like those below. Clearly these are weak inferences which are only more or less consistent with the data. They are not to any interesting extent "proved" by the numbers we have given.

> The chances of getting rich are kind of slim and most people will not make it.
>
> It's not simple, not quick, not effortless, for most of us.
>
> If there are a large number of people trying to get rich, they appear not to be succeeding. Most current approaches aren't working.
>
> If getting rich quick was a process which could be simply and easily explained, if all of the stock market books of the decade of the sixties were right, surely there would be more rich folks.
>
> It's very unlikely to "just happen." We need to stop supposing that somehow we'll come up with the money for college, for health care emergencies, and for retirement.
>
> Most of the rich got there by being remembered in someone's will. Those who got rich quick must be in the remaining minority, and there is little direct evidence as to their methods.
>
> Generally speaking, propositions which promise quick wealth for sure have a very low probability of success.

It would probably be healthy to put in perspective all of our preconceptions about:

The myths and folklore of the rich,

How well off the Joneses really are,

The guy who knows a guy who just made a real killing,

The books on your broker's shelf which will show you how to make it quick for sure,

The gentle innocence of supposing that someday our ship will come in.

Designing Your Targets

A revealing step in coming to understand the GRS hypothesis is to ask yourself the seemingly silly question, "How much do I really want to get rich?" Most people would agree that they want wealth, but the question is more sophisticated than that. How much effort are you willing to exert, how much risk are you willing to assume, how much present consumption are you willing to postpone, how long are you willing to wait to achieve $10,000, or $100,000, or $1,000,000? Clearly all this requires more introspection than most of us find natural. We'll have to look into this more seriously later on when we have some better idea of what's involved. For now, a few questions to get you thinking. Don't try too hard to give yourself firm answers at this point.

To what degree are you willing to do it slowly, if this will substantially increase your chances of success?

How would you choose if you had to select *one* of the following as a way of using all your funds:

Taking a flyer which had a very, very small chance of producing $100,000 in a few months.

Setting out on a program which had a very big chance of producing $100,000 in 20 years.

Undertaking a program which seemed almost certain to produce $10,000 in 10 years.

How far ahead do you ordinarily plan? Does it make any sense to think five or ten years ahead when so many things could upset one's plans?

Are you interested in "having a lot of money" or do you have some pretty clear ideas as to what you want to do with money?

Have you developed some rough estimates of the amount of money you'd like to have to:

solve a health problem in your family?

educate the kids?

buy a bigger home?

travel all over Europe?

take care of your mother?

buy a farm and get away from the rat race?

retire to a mobile home in Florida or Arizona?

How would you rank the items on your own list of wants in the order of their importance to you?

Are you operating under the unconscious, unspoken assumption that someday, somehow, you'll be able to have the things you really want?

Have you given up entirely the notion of getting rich? Does it seem absolutely ridiculous with your income and your obligations to even think about accumulating $10,000 or $100,000?

It is innocent indeed to suppose that good, satisfying answers can be quickly given to such questions. One seldom knows this much about one's self without a good deal of study. There is a lot of evidence to indicate that most people, most companies, most institutions don't know what they want. That is, they don't know what they want with sufficient clarity to make the really difficult and important decisions that matter. Don't be surprised if you decide that you don't know what you want as well as you wish you did. Do, however,

consider a variety of possible goals,

recognize that your wants will change,

mull over the idea that what you want must be related to the time, effort, risk, and luck involved in various methods of achievement.

We will return to these matters in Chapter 8.

A Few Minutes With the Compound Interest Tables

Recently, a noted financial advisor announced that the compound interest tables were the young investor's best friend. They ought, in fact, to be everybody's good friend, since they reveal some surprising and non-intuitive secrets about getting rich slowly. Compound interest, for most of us, is a rather dull topic which came up somewhere in school, but was promptly forgotten because it had something to do with bonds or annuities, which were quite clearly for old people. Quite without fascination at the time. A compound interest situation is simply one where we continually reinvest the interest or return on our capital. At the end of the first year of an investment program, perhaps it earns some return. We invest this return right back in the program. At the end of the second year we get a return on our original investment, plus a return on the first year's return. All of this goes right back into the program. During the third year we have our original capital working, our first year's interest, and our second year's interest which is larger than the first year's. Thus at the end of the third year the return is still larger, and so on and on. Interest, interest on the interest, interest on the interest on the interest. Things tend to mount up this way quite a lot faster than one would expect.

To see how fast, let's look at a few cases. In order to keep it simple, let's suppose that we neglect taxes or assume that taxes are paid from other sources. But let's not forget that these calculations don't include taxes. Actually we will stick to some fairly modest rates of return which are not at all out of the question as "after tax" returns. The tax depends a lot on how you make the money as well as what else you're doing for income, as you know only too well.

Suppose you had the idea that getting rich for you meant getting together a capital fund of $100,000. What kind of money would you have to put into your financial program every year in order to achieve this? Suppose you felt that you could manage your investment in such a way as to have a high probability of achieving a 10 percent return more or less consistently. Table 1–2 indicates that you would have to invest $6,275 each year if you wanted to reach your objective in 10

Table 1-2

ANNUAL SAVINGS NEEDED TO PRODUCE $100,000

COMPOUNDING RATE	Planning Horizon			
	5 YEARS	10 YEARS	15 YEARS	20 YEARS
5%	$18,097	$7,950	$4,634	$3,024
10%	16,380	6,275	3,147	1,746
15%	14,830	4,930	2,100	980
20%	13,440	3,850	1,390	540

years. You would put in a total of $62,750, and the rest of the $100,000 would be the return which you earned over the years, typically from some combination of price appreciation and dividends if you had a stock portfolio. You pick a compounding rate which could be more or less consistently achieved, and a planning horizon, and Table 1–2 will tell you what it will be necessary to invest every year.

If your objective is $10,000, divide it all by ten. If you want to be a millionaire, multiply it all by ten (and remember we have left out taxes). Notice that the numbers in the table are neither proportional nor linear. If you double the planning horizon, for example, this doesn't simply cut the amount to be invested in half. It's these non-linear effects which make the table worth studying for a while. A little playing around with these numbers will give you a much better idea of what kind of trade-off between time and financial objective is reasonable and comfortable for you. I'll have lots to say later on about how to consistently achieve various compounding rates and how to consider the probability that you will succeed.

Table 1–3 takes a different look at the possibilities for getting rich

Table 1-3

Disposable Income After Taxes: **$8,000**
Annual Net Savings: **$ 400**

COMPOUNDING RATE	Planning Horizon			
	5 YEARS	10 YEARS	15 YEARS	20 YEARS
5%	$2,210	$ 5,031	$ 8,632	$13,226
10%	2,442	6,374	12,709	22,910
15%	2,697	8,114	19,048	40,816
20%	2,976	10,389	28,777	74,074

slowly. Economists suggest that the average family with a disposable net income after taxes of $8,000 saves about $400 of this amount. Thus we are looking at the possibilities such an average family has for getting rich, always assuming that nothing happens to disturb their savings program. If, for example, such a family undertook a 20-year program of investing in stocks, and was able to achieve a rather modest

10 percent annual return, they would have accumulated a capital fund of $22,910. Recall that they are saving only $400 per year. Clearly this requires a lot of persistence and this, of course, is the very ingredient we often lack. It is also what much of the rest of this book is about.

Table 1–4 gives you the same kind of information for the average

Table 1-4

Disposable Income After Taxes: **$10,000**
Annual Net Savings: **$ 1,170**

COMPOUNDING RATE	Planning Horizon			
	5 YEARS	10 YEARS	15 YEARS	20 YEARS
5%	$6,465	$14,716	$25,247	$ 38,687
10%	7,142	18,646	37,173	67,012
15%	7,889	23,732	55,714	119,388
20%	8,705	30,390	84,172	216,667

family with $10,000 of disposable income after taxes. Such a family typically saves $1,170 a year. If they simply went down to the corner savings and loan for a sure 5%, they would have enough in 15 years to fully finance the college education of a couple of children. Table 1–5 does the same thing for the $12,000-after-tax income family. If they invested in a moderately good mutual fund which achieved the equivalent of 15 percent annual return, they would have over $100,000 in 15 years. But again, the key is sticking to it.

These compounding effects usually come as something of a surprise to those who have not had their couple of minutes with tables of this kind. If you make more money than these few examples cover, get a set of compound interest tables and work out some numbers appropriate to your situation. You may be astonished at the possibilities for achieving a quarter of a million or half a million dollars. Compounding effects constitute one of the least appreciated aspects of the GRS hypothesis. It is essential in developing your financial program to have a feel for just how rich it is possible to get with modest inputs and modest rates of return, IF you are willing to do it slowly. For some useful tables, see pages 119 and 120.

Table 1-5

Disposable Income After Taxes: $12,000
Annual Net Savings: $ 2,150

COMPOUNDING RATE	Planning Horizon			
	5 YEARS	10 YEARS	15 YEARS	20 YEARS
5%	$11,881	$27,043	$ 46,395	$ 71,092
10%	13,126	34,265	68,310	123,141
15%	14,498	43,611	102,381	219,389
20%	15,997	55,844	154,676	398,148

Let's keep giving all of this a very hard-nosed look. You've got to;

consistently, relentlessly make the annual investments,

think in terms of years, not weeks or months,

have it very clear in your mind that the higher the compounding rate you try for, the greater are the chances you will fail.

After you have studied the compound interest tables awhile you'll be able to work out some more complicated and realistic programs. For example, if you already have $5,000, and invest it and in addition put $100 a month into a stock portfolio for ten years, a 15% rate will produce almost $45,000. Or consider a young family with a typical professional such as an engineer at its head. Based on average incomes, such a family might reasonably save $80 a month for the first five years, $160 a month for the next five, and $240 a month for the next ten. If they could achieve an annual return of only 10%, they would have a capital fund of $100,000 at the end of this 20-year period.

The Chances of Success

The chances of making one of these rates of return, that is, *actually* doing it, depend in part on you and in part on the market or whatever it is you're in. I will try to show you that they depend much more on you than on the market and try to work out some effective ways to improve these chances. But just to get an initial feel and to suggest the way in which the market behaves, let's look at some of the chances of making the kind of return that has been used in these examples. Right now (1973), one could get 6% at a savings and loan bank and 8% on pretty good corporate bonds. (Remember we are still neglecting taxes.) Most people feel that the risk involved at these levels is minimal, and that the probability of consistently achieving these returns is very high indeed. Thus if you are planning a program involving a 6 to 8 percent rate of return, you might be willing to say that the probability of the market doing its part to achieve your objective is nearly one. This has to be combined with the probability that you will do your part.

When we get above the yield on corporate bonds, we are talking about the stock market and considering combinations of price appreciation and dividend income. There is lots and lots of data on market performance around. The actual numbers depend very heavily on what particular time period you're talking about. For example, the 10 years ending in 1968 usually look a good deal different from the 10 years ending in 1969. Furthermore, you have to make your peace with the question of how the market's performance of the past is related to that of the future. Recognize then that the data about the past is but one ingredient in the reduction of your uncertainty about the outcome of your financial plans. However, it is a good ingredient with which to begin because it polices your ideas for any of the misconceptions about the market we tend to pick up. There is so much of this kind of information readily available that we will only give a small sample:

In 1972, half of the companies in the country earned more than 12% return on their shareholders' equity.

A study of 34 mutual funds for the period 1954–1963 showed returns varying from 10 percent to 19 percent.

A famous study has compared the performance of 136 mutual funds with the average performance of randomly selected portfolios generated from 511 stocks traded on the New York Stock Exchange. The interesting results shown in Table 1–6 are typical.

Taking a look at literally all of the common stock funds which have been listed in Wiesenberger's *Investment Companies* indicates the order of magnitude of their average performance. If, for example, we choose a 15-year period, assume an 8.5 percent sales charge, and assume reinvestment of all dividends and distributions (we continue to leave out taxes) we get something like Table 1–7.

Table 1-6

Period	Mutual Funds	Random Porfolios
Jan 1960- Mar 1964	9.0%	7.0%
Apr 1964- June 1968	12.8%	17.8%
Jan 1960- June 1968	10.7%	12.4%

Table 1-7

FOR THE 15-YEAR PERIOD ENDING IN:	ANNUAL RATE OF RETURN TO NEAREST PERCENT:
1964	12 %
1965	13
1966	11
1967	13
1968	11
1969	9
1970	8
1971	10

One advisory service that follows no-load mutual funds supplies data like the following:

from the May 1970 low to the November 1971 low, a period of about 18 months;

the Dow Jones Industrial Average increased by 26%,

a group of 8 "aggressive" funds increased by 84%,

a group of 6 somewhat less aggressive funds increased by 55%.

Other advice appearing in a leading business magazine says that one can reasonably expect long term performance of 10 to 11 percent from conservative funds and relatively secure 12 to 13 percent from the more aggressive funds.

Your broker may well have a list of stocks which, over long periods, have produced average results of 20%, 40%, and much more. Just let him know you're interested in such things.

Clearly you can turn up an almost unlimited supply of such data, and we are not going to attempt any grand compilation of it here. But in working with it, perhaps you will want to consider several points.

There seem to be a very great many ways you could have made 10 percent, somewhat fewer ways you could have made 20 percent and so on. But you would have had to actually make the commitments, to have been in the market, to have stuck it out through the ups and downs.

This data doesn't age very well, it is very sensitive to the time period considered and the assumptions one makes. Its best use is to give one a general impression of the probabilities of achieving various levels of performance. It clearly indicates that returns in the 10 to 20 percent region are quite possible. To me it indicates that they are also quite probable, if I can only have the self-control to make the necessary commitment.

Whenever one looks at averages, it is important to reflect that about half of the funds or stocks studied did better than the average, and about half did worse. Thus if you had chosen at random one of the opportunities studied, your chances of doing better than the average would have been about 50 percent. With any selectivity, advice, or attentiveness at all, your chances of being above the average seem to me to be greater than 50 percent.

Stocks, funds, and portfolios go up and down. Some fluctuate, some go down and stay there, and some go up and stabilize. When you're considering the usual discussions of volatility and risk, keep in mind that there can be a big difference between studies which evaluate performance over arbitrary periods of time and what you would actually do if you were selling out your portfolio. If you are concerned that you might have to sell out at some point in time to meet a totally unforseen obligation, then you should be concerned about the probabilities that your portfolio will be up or down. The usual measures of risk, average annual fluctuation or standard deviation of annual performance, are interesting if you have to sell at a point not of your own choosing. But the basic idea of a GRS plan is to be able to anticipate the need to sell, to switch when it seems wise, and to wait for the gains which you expect. For example, if you want to build a fund for college expenses or retirement, you have some leeway, perhaps a couple of years either way, as to when you liquidate your portfolio and spend the money or put it into bonds. The market drop of 1969 was serious only if you had to liquidate and use the money at the bottom. If you can choose your time to move, you clearly have very much higher probabilities of achievement than are suggested by most of the standard statistical studies.

You should look at the GRQ (get rich quick) data, too, the stocks that doubled or tripled in a year. There usually aren't too many, but almost always enough to make one nervous. Which ones will double or triple next year?

The Crucial Experiment

Perhaps you are sort of with me at this point, willing to agree that most firms, individuals, and institutions who got rich on their own did it slowly, deliberately, and consistently. Their successes attracted nothing like the notice which came to the very few who did it quickly. Maybe you're willing to concede that if you could be strong, persistent, and self-disciplined, the chances of getting rich slowly are very high. Maybe you agree that this "if" is a very big "if" indeed, and that if this book is going to amount to anything, it will have to deal at great length with how to increase the probability that you will do what is required. Maybe you are willing to agree that if a plan can be developed for testing the GRS hypothesis, you'd be willing to have a go at it.

Don't trust yourself. Don't be insulted if I say I don't trust you at this point. Not that you'd deliberately deceive either of us.

A prerequisite which is essential to undertaking a GRS program is a conviction, based on actual experience, that *You* are most unlikely to get rich quickly. Without this conviction, arising out of actual experience, most of us are stuck with a residual feeling that we could be one of the chosen few. In spite of all the probabilities, in spite of all the reasonable reflection, there are people who do get rich quickly and we might just be among them. This residual feeling tempts us to try things repeatedly, is almost sure to upset any GRS plan we make, and leaves us easy marks for the steady stream of GRQ schemes which come along. Nothing is more important than to find out if we can get rich quickly by giving it a try. But equally important is to give it a try in a way which will maximize what we learn and not blow the whole financial future of the family. Thus, the GRQ experiment.

2

Paying the Tuition: The GRQ Experiment

Strange advice. There are some things we can learn ↵
only from experience. If we need to know them, we
need to get the experience deliberately and carefully.
How to try getting rich quickly and get the most out
of the attempt. Not rich . . . but perhaps smart.

To Begin, Drop a Bundle

The data, such as it is, on how the rich got to be rich, leaves us with
an annoying void. Most of them inherited wealth, but we just don't
know much about how the others did it. Presumably some did indeed
get rich quickly.

Perhaps there are an interesting number who did it "overnight" and
perhaps you have whatever it may take to join them. While for most
people the chances of getting rich quick are infinitesimally small, for
you and the deals you run into, they might seem much higher. High
enough to warrant a try. Perhaps at this point you freeze, you can't
quite bring yourself to try one of those wild propositions. **Try it.** Try

it just as soon as you're convinced it's worth a try. Don't wait around. Muster up your courage and have a go. But do it in a way that will maximize your payoff. Do it in a way which will permit you to explain the value of the results to yourself and your spouse, no matter how it turns out.

Clearly, I'm urging you to go out and blow a chunk of your capital, because I'm convinced that your chances of any other result in a good honest attempt to get rich quick are not zero, but pretty close to zero. The whole idea of urging people to deliberately take a plunge seems strange to many, but what I have in mind is a special kind of plunge. Not casual, not haphazard, but a rather carefully designed experiment: the GRQ experiment.

Why?

No matter what your intellectual view of the chances of getting rich quickly are, if you haven't really tried it you probably don't have the mental set which will give you a high chance of success in a GRS program. If you haven't made a real attempt to double or triple your money in a few months, if you haven't actually taken a flyer at whatever it is you think will do it for you, the GRQ experiment should be your next step. I have no way of getting proof; but I have hypothesized that many of the really effective professionals in the financial world have made this experiment somewhere along the line, and that an important dimension of their professional competence results from it.

It is possible that some of us have an intuitive sense of the market which will lead to quick wealth. It is possible that some of us have "systems" which will do the same. It is even possible that once in your life you will pick the one stock which will solve completely all of your financial problems. These things are indeed possible and the possibilities are so tempting, so potentially distracting that they need to be tested; tested not with make-believe simulations in the stock market tables, but with real and substantial amounts of money. Unless one has put an interesting sum on the rumor, the hunch, the tip, the inside deal, or whatever it is that looks like a GRQ opportunity, one lacks the kind of understanding that comes only from living through it. Unless one has experienced the discouragement, the frustration, the bitterness, the remorse, the explanations, and the rationalizations which follow failure, one lacks the essential turn of mind to succeed in a GRS program.

This is the way, the only way for most of us, to purge that residue of doubt. Few others will get rich quickly, but I'm smarter, or luckier, or better informed, or better connected, so I'm different. Until we've really "taken a bath," this residual doubt is very likely to trap us. It will almost surely prevent us from getting rich at all. We must subject ourselves to an experience of sufficient motivational and financial impact to make the chances of getting rich quickly seem so small that they are useless. We need to arrive at a state of mind which will condition us to ignore GRQ propositions in the future. Thinking about it, reading about it, or getting simulated experience just will not do it for most of us.

In my view, your GRQ experiment is almost certain to be a financial failure. You probably won't learn very much about the stock market in the process either. But you will learn a very great deal about yourself and your responses to GRQ opportunities, to real market situations, and to the frustrations of losses. It's just possible, of course, that you will get rich quickly when you make the experiment. If this happens, take all of your money immediately to a bank and hire a trust officer to manage it for you. Tell him to permit you an income, but under no conditions whatever, to let you get back into the market with the bulk of your funds. The chances of doing it once seem to me very, very small. The chances of doing it twice in a row are many orders of magnitude smaller.

Designing the Experiment

Right here, and all the way through the discussion which follows, I run into an old and difficult problem. If I tell someone that they should change their natural, habitual way of doing something, they will resist the idea. Trying to get someone to change the way they do their job or manage their affairs is almost sure to fail if you approach them as the expert who can show them how they really should be doing it. People resist change, interpret your suggestions as criticisms, and become even more convinced that their own way is the best. The classic way of dealing with this problem is to try to stimulate people to be interested in the general idea of change and improvement, but to let them work out their own new patterns of behavior. If you can get a man to invent for himself new ways of doing his job, he doesn't feel criticised, his ego isn't threatened, and he's likely to actually change his behavior.

Similarly, if I tell you that you ought to get busy and make a GRQ experiment, if I specify in great detail how you ought to do this, if I tell you exactly how to interpret the results, the chances of your actually doing anything are minimal. On the other hand if I can get you interested in what you have to gain from a GRQ experiment, get you interested in designing your own, and have you, not me, interpret the results, then something may actually happen. What I will try to do as best I can, both here and in subsequent chapters, is tell you enough to get you interested in working things out for yourself. If I can say just enough about a GRQ experiment to move you to sit down and design your own, then there is a good chance you'll actually carry out your experiment, a good chance that you'll learn a lot from it, and a good chance that you'll go ahead to get rich slowly.

So as you read on, think about designing your own GRQ experiment and don't try to guess what I have in mind. I will set down some things which I think are important, but the most important thing of all is that you develop your own plans and actually carry them out.

Experience and Experiment

Experimental design in science has a fundamental common sense quality about it which is seldom very obvious to those who learn about science through the popular press. Scientists write things down so they will remember them and remember them accurately. They decide in advance just what an experiment is supposed to test, being quite clear *in advance* as to what conclusions they will draw from the various experimental outcomes which can be anticipated. It is surprisingly easy to do experiments without being very sure when they are over, what they proved. It is even easier after the results are in, to fall, quite unconsciously, into an interpretation of them which serves one's needs or expectations. Things like these are the real strength of experimentation as a source of information, as opposed to casual experience. While it is important to learn from experience, that experience should be planned if it is to be efficient. What usually passes for experience is likely to be fairly wasteful as an information gathering method. These common sense things are what we aim for in designing a GRQ experiment.

Step 1—The Hypothesis

Decide in advance what exactly it is that you believe about yourself and the market. Notice that we are planning an experiment that involves both. For example;

I have the intuition, skill, or natural ability to really make it big on my hunches. I will be able to double or triple my funds every few months.

I have some really important information, not already widely known or appreciated, that I can use to multiply my capital by a factor of 10.

I can consistently achieve an annual performance on the order of 50 percent, simply by following the system which I have discovered.

This advisory service picked seven stocks which doubled in six months. I am going to follow their advice and do the same in the next six months.

My broker likes me and is giving me the really hot ideas.

I'm just going to take a blind shot.

If George can do it, so can I.

Puts and calls, warrants, or convertibles are the way to do it. Look at what you could have done last year.

The biggest play is in the commodity market. If I read enough about it, I can get in on it, too.

The idea here is to decide as clearly as you can what hypothesis about you and the market you are testing. Otherwise when it's all over you may not know exactly what the results of your experiment mean.

Step 2—Anticipate the Results

Decide in advance, while you are calm and before you get involved in interpreting and rationalizing, what it would take to convince you. What would it take to bring you to the conclusion that you should try again on the basis of your GRQ hypothesis? What would it take for you to conclude that so little credibility should be attached to your hypothesis as to make it useless as a basis for further financial operations? How many times would you have to try? How many different hypotheses would you want to investigate? Look at yourself carefully and make a firm commitment. For example;

If I can't really make it big once in x tries, I don't have it.

If I don't double my money in y months, I don't have it.

Make a clear determination, in advance, of what you think would be a reasonable reaction to the various ways your experiment could turn out. If you wait until after the results are in, you're almost sure to kid yourself about what happened and rationalize it to others.

Step 3—Write, Write, Write

Most beginners keep all sorts of records of the market and what their stocks are doing. What is important is to keep records of what you are doing. Make a written record of all that you have concluded in Step 1 and Step 2. The experiment *must* be based on a written plan, which will not only help your memory, but will tend to insulate you from all the forces which distract you from what you set out to do. Keep a record of what you decide and why you decide it. Don't be casual about it, writing on the backs of old envelopes. Be a scientist with a bound notebook in which you write carefully and date your entries. Keep the notebook handy most of the time. The GRQ experiment is likely to be expensive and this notebook is going to be the most useful result of it.

Step 4—Make It Hurt

Make a deliberate and careful decision as to how much money it will take to convince you of the results. The more money you lose the more firmly the experience will be impressed on your mind and the longer the good effects will last. The idea is to find the amount of money which will really hurt, which will overcome your tendency to rationalize, which will really purge your residual doubts about getting rich quick. Get in for enough money to insure that the loss is likely to remove the last shred of future temptation.

Only you can figure out what this amount is, and you may have to try a couple of times before you find the answer. To lose a few dollars will hardly teach you anything. To lose your entire capital fund may teach you something, but it will leave you without the means to profit from what you have learned. Divide up your funds so that when the experiment fails, you'll have something to go on with. Don't necessarily commit everything in one plunge; perhaps you will want to plan a series of smaller experiments whose total impact is significant. But above all, avoid the tendency to blow all you have, no matter how great your GRQ hypothesis looks. The least sensible experiments are those which are designed on the basis of the "there's no tomorrow" hypothesis.

Have a clear recovery plan for after the experiment. Your reserve funds must be absolutely inviolate to GRQ schemes.

Finally—What to Watch For

When your experiment is over, either head for the bank with your wealth or sit down with your notebook. What kind of rationalizations are you tempted to give?

I was deliberately cheated.

Something happened which nobody could possibly have foreseen.

I had to give up the experiment because the stock went down and I couldn't get out without a loss.

My judgment was good, but the advice I got from my broker, my advisory service, or my barber, was lousy.

Everybody lost a lot of money during this period, so I can hardly be blamed for what happened.

This one didn't pay off, but how about trying for two out of three?

I started off as a trader, but when the market went down I became an investor.

That notebook with my original hypothesis and design in it is pretty childish. The really big operators don't do that kind of thing.

I'm getting out of the market entirely and forever. From here on it's government bonds and the savings and loan.

If my spouse would only let me try it once more, I'm sure I could do it.

I was on vacation when the market broke.

You'll think of lots more ways of trying to go easy on yourself. Why not face the fact that you lost your money but really got a big bargain. If you got rid of that residual belief in the chances of getting rich quick, you're now ready to undertake a GRS program. You've substantially increased the probability that you'll be able to carry out such a program, and thus substantially increased your chances of ending up rich.

You may also learn a few things about yourself. Are you a worrier? Did you panic when things went to pieces? Did you refuse to believe that things just were not working out the way you were certain they were going to? Did you go into it without any explicit expression of the uncertainty with which you viewed it? Did you get miserable with your family as things went from bad to worse? Did you keep clutching for reasons why it was all going to turn out fine in the end? Did you lie awake nights? Did your effectiveness on the job go down? Did you stop bragging about your financial operations and get very evasive when somebody asked? Did your self-image as a really bright, cool, big-time market operator give way to a feeling that you are a real idiot?

Keep track of these observations in your notebook. Writing them down may even help to relieve some of the guilt, frustration, and anxiety that you feel. Their sharpness will fade quickly, and it will be not only interesting, but wonderfully useful to read them over from time to time. Don't let your research notebook get lost. We'll be using it frequently from here on out.

After the GRQ experiment is over, take a few weeks off. Then start on the program which will give you a very good chance of getting rich slowly.

3

Stock Market Research and Advice

Messages from the PhD's and their computers. Reading the charts and taking random walks. Fundamentalists, students of folklore, and dart throwers can all make money. So can contrarians and formula planners. The hardnosed treatment for your advisory service. It's easy and profitable to be about average.

Waves From the Great Beyond

"Heavy transits of Jupiter and Saturn continued to drive the market down this week." Advisory services have prospered from the sale of advice based on astrological considerations and on the interpretation of signals given by the comic strips. The mystery of it all, coupled with a need to have someone else make our decisions for us, perhaps spiced with a couple of examples of how you might have made money, seems to assure that most any kind of advisory service can find, at least, a brief following. Mass psychology is influenced by the changing potential in the electrical energy field of the solar system because our minds are electrical transformers. So goes the underlying logic of an advisory ser-

31

vice which is available for several hundred dollars a year. This particular service predicted on November 20, 1968 that the market would end its long upward trend over the weekend of December 2. It actually ended on December 3 with the Dow Jones Industrial Average at 985. Luck or skill? Dependable, reliable, or just a fluke? If you had followed this advice you would have done better financially than the vast majority of professionals. This sort of thing makes many of us uneasy. On the one hand, it sounds a little too implausible to put any money on. On the other hand, the persistent feeling that we may be missing out on something very good indeed will make subscribers out of some of us. Even Wall Street professionals do not always brush aside these predictions. The investment chairman of one major firm and a partner of another both commented favorably in the press on the track record of this particular service. Some clear thinking is needed to undo this ambivalence.

Like the basement inventor who has been replaced by the corporate product development group, stock market research is no longer a cottage industry. Working long into the night charting one's own stock market data has (or really should have) lost the flicker of hope which kept many of us at it. Research on the market has become highly technical, very expensive, and largely the province of PhD's liberally endowed with digital computer time. Generally speaking, brokers and advisory services are not equipped to deal at this level and, as a result, show a considerable tendency to give it bad notices. The results of this very sophisticated work are largely available in the open literature to anyone who can read it. What is required is not much more than a modest background in probability theory and statistics. Yet if one is willing to forego the details, it is perfectly possible to catch the general message that this research has about the workings of the market without such a background. Indeed, before one undertakes any of those long evenings with his own special schemes for plotting prices and volumes, it would be revealing to have a look at just a bit of the very large amount of work that has been done since the advent of the computer.

Today's research climate presents one with a puzzle. It is a puzzle which is not only intriguing, but probably contains an essential clue needed to understand the systems approach to getting rich slowly but almost surely. The PhD's who are doing the new research don't give much outward evidence that they are getting rich rapidly. Yet what they are saying is that the approaches which have been long used by many market professionals are almost sure to be useless. The professionals' ideas about the market have been, in many cases, shown to be hopeless as *consistent* methods of achieving better than average performance. The professionals are generally cool toward these findings and sometimes have a good laugh over them. The professionals, indeed, give every outward appearance of going right on making satisfying amounts of money with the very methods that the digital computers have shown to be highly unreliable. This is doubtless a complex contradiction, but we may be able to offer a plausible and useful explanation, an explanation which indicates the sort of thing the professionals know that most of us don't. Thankfully, we can learn it. First, however, a quick look at a few approaches to the market and what the computer and the PhD's have done to them.

The Broadening Top, The Falling Wedge, The Head and Shoulders Bottom

Technical analysis preys on those tantalizing regularities which we think we see in graphs of stock prices and trading volumes. It gives those patterns names; the "head and shoulders bottom," and so on. The names make them seem even more appealing, more scientific, and more authoritative. If one appreciates an imaginative attempt at imposing order on stock price data, a good book on technical analysis makes exciting reading. Many of these patterns can be associated with plausible stories about what is going on in the minds of those who are in the market, stories which add still another dimension of profundity to the work of the technician. There are a couple of problems, however. Technical analysis is extremely difficult to test directly. There are several practical reasons for this. Technicians have named a very large number of patterns, and what you may think is pattern A with bullish implications, another technician may confidently identify as Pattern B with the opposite implications. Further, the catalog of patterns often includes both, say, a "head and shoulders bottom" and a "false head and shoulders bottom," which are extremely difficult to distinguish, except on graphs of what happened last year. Technicians seldom make any explicit statements at all of the reliability of their patterns. This is quite understandable, however, since the work was done long before we had the computers which would be needed to handle anything like the required amount of data. See page 121 for an example.

Technical analysis is a good example of the need to test the operationality of a market approach. Can it actually be used? That is, can it actually be used by someone who has read the book and understood the explicit parts of the method? Technicians usually suggest that their work requires experience, judgment, skill, or some other such ingredient which cannot, of course, be transmitted simply by instruction. A most valuable exercise indeed is to sit down with a book on technical analysis and a current chart of one's favorite stock, and try to determine exactly what pattern is being traced out by the stock as it traded today, yesterday, and last week. The patterns are wonderfully clear when someone has drawn the lines over the charts from years past, but to say what is presently going on in these terms is hopelessly ambiguous for most of us. The test of operationality, "Can *you* actually use it?" is surprisingly often failed by the widely discussed approaches to the market. It's a test which you should always make for yourself, since the real question is whether *you* can use a particular scheme. See page 128.

The Random Walk Hypothesis

The hope that by looking at past price movements, one could reliably predict future price movements must run deep in many of us. Technical analysis has enjoyed a long history without really having to justify itself. Technicians appear to go right on making money. The difficulty of testing the hypothesis directly was, however, finally overcome by the combined forces of probability theory and the computer. For some time now, the random walk hypothesis has been one of the topics which could raise the temperature of most any market discussion. You can easily produce a random walk of your own for study.

Put your pencil in the center of the left hand side of a piece of graph paper and start flipping an ordinary coin. Every time you get a "head" move the pencil one square to the right and then one square up. Every time you get a "tail" move the pencil one square to the right and one square down. Your pencil will execute one sort of random walk, and the resulting graph will allow you to study its path. As you look at the graph you're almost sure to see regular trends up or down, some well-behaved waves, or some other surprisingly orderly formation. You've just become a technical analyst. Now think about the coin. Having no memory, it cannot regulate its behavior on the basis of what it has done in the past.

A head or a tail, an up or a down, always have the same probability. Even if we've just had ten successive heads (ups), the chance of a head on the eleventh flip is still the same. This worries some people who have mistaken notions about what they call "the law of averages," but a little thought about how the coin remembers what it has done and the history of coins which you pull out of your pocket, will usually serve to convince them. Technically speaking, we say that the outcome of the eleventh flip is independent of the past sequence of heads and tails. Practically speaking, we would say that knowing what the coin has done in the past is of no additional help in predicting what it will do in the future.

Now if you were to think of your random walk graph as a stock price chart, you would be saying that past price changes offer no additional help in predicting future price changes. Or you could say the price change tomorrow is independent of the price change today. It is important to notice that we are talking about price changes, not the actual prices themselves. The PhD's have made some very elaborate statistical tests of all this, using very large amounts of data in their computers. They have come to the conclusion that it is not unreasonable to think of stock prices as random walks, and stock price changes as being independent. When one talks in general terms about technical things, there is every possibility that the specifics will be imperfectly communicated. You should read about the random walk hypothesis in detail if you're interested, and you'll discover that there are lots of "if's" and "but's" involved. The general notion, however, is that stock price changes look very much like random processes and thus it is reasonable to take the view that stock prices behave as if they were random walks. For a given stock, the probability distribution of tomorrow's price change is the same as the probability distribution for the day after tomorrow. See page 128.

Nobody is saying that price changes are controlled by some great coin flipper in the sky; only that from all we can tell, price changes behave as if they were random and independent. Put another way, if several random walks were plotted on the same sort of paper as several actual stock price series and then mixed up, there would be no reliable way of telling which graphs were stocks and which were not. There is a great deal of evidence to support this conclusion. Of course, if you believe it, there's no future at all in technical analysis. The research may need some refinements, but it seems clear that if there is anything at all to technical analysis, it is so tenuous, so unreliable, as to be completely useless for profitable market operations. There is little opportunity for profit in the study of past price movements, and further research of a technical nature is probably not going to be fruitful. Naturally the professional technicians who give all sorts of appearances of making money think all this is nuts.

If, however, you come to accept the random walk hypothesis after you've looked into it a little further, then a real breath of fresh air blows into your life. All that complex messing around with price and volume charts is not going to be of consistent help in bringing you better than average performance. You may still wonder, as I do, how come the technicians seem to keep profiting from their mysterious work. Back to this puzzle in Chapter 4.

Fundamentals

Fundamental analysts, very roughly speaking, undertake to forecast a firm's future earnings, consider whether the present price of the firm's stock does or does not reflect these earnings expectations, and predict stock price changes accordingly. There is good evidence to show that changes in earnings are indeed reflected in changes in stock prices, although the relationship is by no means as simple and direct as one might suspect. At least it appears worthwhile to attempt to predict earnings. Unfortunately, it is rather well established by the PhD's and their computers that trying to forecast a company's future earnings by simply extrapolating their past earnings record is not going to be usefully reliable. Fundamentalists look at the firm's management, markets, products, competition, financial structure, research efforts, patents, and many other aspects in attempting to predict earnings. They also consider how the economy, international trade, monetary policy, fiscal policy, and so on, are likely to influence earnings. Unfortunately, they usually do this in what they see as very complex, subtle, judgmental, intuitive ways that cannot really be tested explicitly. Still and all, those who take a fundamental approach to the market and do it professionally, give every appearance, like the technicians, of making money.

Like the technicians also, the fundamentalists have heard from the PhD's. In March of 1972 three professors from a prominent Ivy League school made the headlines by announcing that fundamental analysis was not terribly useful. They implied, without explaining very fully, that they had done better than nineteen professionally managed portfolios by throwing darts into the stock market pages of their newspapers. The fundamentalists responded predictably, offering their track records to support their refusal to believe the professors.

Random Portfolios

We slipped by some data that appears in Chapter 2 without comment, indicating that the average performance of some randomly selected portfolios was better than the average performance of a large number of professionally managed mutual funds. Here again as with the Ivy League professors, we encounter that same interesting comparison. Congress, always looking sharply at the financial community, has recently come upon the notion that "dart throwing" may be just as effective as professional management and made the expected declarations of shock and alarm.

What is interesting is not whether one randomly selected portfolio outperforms the professionals, since this only shows that it is possible. We knew this in advance. The real question is "What is the probability that a randomly generated portfolio will outperform a given professionally managed portfolio?" It would take a study of a large number of random portfolios to get a first cut at this probability. If it turns out that a large proportion of random portfolios outperform a large number of professionally managed ones, then we might as well conclude that it is very difficult for the professionals to achieve outstanding results. It is relatively easy for anyone to achieve results comparable with the professionals.

If the average of a large number of random portfolios is close to the performance of a given professional portfolio, then we might conclude that the dart throwing business is about as likely to be better as it is likely to be worse. If this appears to be the case, then it might be very reasonable to question the value of the professional management. Before you do this, make sure that you've looked at at least ten years performance of both. And before you turn your back on the professionals, think about what you're going to do.

If you're about to swing into some careful portfolio selection process yourself, you will be trying to do what the professionals do, and you will, of course, be contradicting yourself. If the professionals can't do better than random selection, then neither can you. The thing to do then is to get the stock market tables up on the wall and start throwing darts. Think about that. How many darts? How much of your money on each stock thus selected? Will you really be able to take your hard-earned dollars down to the broker's office and put in the buy orders? If your portfolio shoots up or shoots down, will you panic? If you can do these things, there is a high probability (in my view) that you will make money over the long term. There is (also in my view) a good probability that you will do better than a lot of professionally managed portfolios. But the question is, "Can you do your part?" Can you actually throw the darts, commit the funds, and hang in there? This may be the thing that the pros can do and the amateurs can't do.

Trading Folklore

There are a host of fascinating assertions about regularities in the behavior of the market to which many of us are almost hopelessly addicted. The Summer rally, the year-end tax selling. Sell on the rumor of a strike but buy on the news of a strike. Rising volume accompanying rising prices is bullish. All of this wisdom is picked up and remembered because it gives one a feeling of intimacy, of really knowing the market. It is rich enough to explain anything that may happen, and, indeed, research directors of major brokerage firms repeat it daily in those little quotes that accompany the stock market story in the paper. Nothing much is ever said about the reliability of these supposed regularities, probably because until the computer got involved, testing seemed an almost hopeless task. But now the testing process has begun.

Stocks rise in January.

It takes volume to make prices move.

It takes volume to put prices up, but they can fall of their own weight.

Important moves tend to end on large volume. The selling climax, for example.

Rallies from a decline tend to be abrupt, but passage through a peak tends to be more leisurely. The ping-pong ball hypothesis. Volume tends to peak before prices.

This sort of trading folklore has now been studied rather carefully, and the results make interesting reading. Reading that each of us should do for himself. My own impression of the research is that there isn't any very reliable method of profiting from this work. There does, indeed, seem to be something to some of these kinds of statements. The basis, however, seems to be so weak, so tenuous, of such low reliability, that it would be difficult to make much money this way. To take a simple example: Stocks rise in January. Sure enough, if you look at the January's from 1871 to 1968, the Standard and Poor's index did rise 73% of the time. Now try to figure out how long it would take you to get rich using this information. Remember that prices fell in January 27% of the time.

Ten Thousand Ways to Skin a Cat

The creation of theories, methods, philosophies, and systems for approaching the market is an exciting challenge for the intellect. We are probably in for a stream of such ideas that will go on so long as the market itself seems to hold such irresistible and exciting possibilities for profit. Most of those approaches which get sufficiently well developed to be reduced to writing, probably exhibit three common characteristics:

They will appear for brief periods to show exceptionally good, even dramatic performance.

They will have no explicit record of long-run consistent performance.

They will contain some crucial aspects which are not made explicit, not operational, and which are said to involve judgment, experience, or "feel."

Read about them. They are intensely interesting. Some of them seem to be the work of highly creative minds applied with great energy to vast amounts of data. Their creators seem to be men of courage and also men of great insight into the psychology of the market. Even more interesting are the ways in which some of these approaches are attuned to our fears, our weaknesses, and our needs. They meet our need to approach financial operations with seemingly rational methods, our needs to suppress uncertainty by appeal to authority, system, or theory. They satisfy our very human desire to have the really difficult decisions made for us.

A brief and innocent survey of a few more philosophies will help to introduce some basic hypotheses about market approaches generally. The adherents of any particular philosophy will surely find that our statement of their views seriously oversimplifies what they believe. Almost all of those who have a philosophy will urge that it is only a part of their total approach to the market, indicating a little mysteriously, that they use many other considerations in forming their market judgments.

The flow-of-funds folks reason that if the big institutions which dominate the market have money to buy stocks, then the market can go up. If the mutual funds, pension funds, trust funds and so on, do not have money, they cannot buy, and the market will not go up. It is thus important to keep track of the cash positions of these institutions, the net purchases or redemptions of mutual funds, the amount of money people have in savings accounts, and the relative attractiveness of bonds as opposed to stocks. Any company whose outstanding stock is heavily held by mutual funds should be avoided, since if the funds all decide to sell at once, the stock is in for a serious decline. If one can guess what it is that fund managers are going to view next as a turnaround situation, one has an excellent buy, since the resulting demand is almost certain to produce an interesting price appreciation.

A somewhat cynical, but coldly realistic air surrounds those who adopt the hypothesis that the little guy always gets taken and that the public is a bunch of emotional amateurs. These people say that the small investor is almost always wrong and the small investor deals in odd lots. Watch the odd lot data. If the odd lotters are not sellers for an extended period, the market is near a bottom and the thing to do is buy. If the odd lotters are net buyers, they are wrong again. The market is close to a top, and the smart money gets out of stocks. It is probably the case that most small investors now deal in round lots, not odd lots as was once the case. Further, if one looks at the activity of such individual investors over the years, from 1966 through 1972, they were by and large quite successful. There was a good deal of individual investor buying at bottoms and selling at tops, enough to cast some real doubt on the simple minded notion that the little man always loses because the big man always wins.

Classic double thinkers in the market are called contrarians. They feel that the thing to do is to gauge the prevailing attitude of those who are in the market and then do the opposite. The theory of contrary opinion looks not so much at what people are doing, as it does at understanding what the general sentiment is at any moment. Contrarians are like those who watch odd lot figures, in the sense that they believe the public is very likely to be exactly wrong in its attitudes at market tops and bottoms. In the midst of trends, however, the public is usually right. Thus one has the added problem of not only trying to assess what the general opinion is, but where we are in the development of a major market movement. If a trend has most of its run ahead, the public is right, but if a trend is nearing its end, the public is wrong. As with most approaches, all this is conditioned by the observation that the theory of contrary opinion is only one aspect of predicting the market. Contrarians hedge a little bit further, too. They are given to saying that what they want to do is make investors think, question, and consider various possibilities. People who try to use the theory of contrary opinion as a mechanistic guide, they say, miss its real point.

The great dream of the real systemizer is to find the completely mechanistic set of trading rules that can be applied mindlessly for exceptional profit. Systems which can be reduced to formulas of some sort have a very special appeal and dignity. This whole area of research has come to be called formula planning. The simplest such scheme is dollar cost averaging. Buy an equal dollar amount of a stock at fixed time intervals. When the price is high, you will buy relatively fewer shares than when the price is low. This will have the interesting effect of "averaging down" the cost of the shares, and increasing the probability that the portfolio is in the black. The next obvious step is to add to this simple formulation some rule for selling as well as buying. One has to be careful here not to invent a formulation which involves so much buying and selling that one's profits are consumed by the broker's commissions. Thus it seems reasonable to wait until the stock has moved up or down by at least some minimum amount before trading. A rule which has been rather carefully investigated goes this way:

If the price of a stock moves up by x percent, buy and hold until the price falls x percent below a later high. At that point, sell and take a short position. Hold the short position until the price rises above a later low by x percent. Then buy enough to cover and take a long position.

With a nice specific, mechanical rule like this one can use the computer to explore its performance over long periods of time. It doesn't have, once one has chosen a value for x, any vague, judgmental aspects to make the test difficult. This particular rule has been tested on the thirty stocks in the Dow Jones Industrial Average for the five years ending in 1962. Values of x from 0.5 percent up to 20.0 percent were tested. With the smallest value of x, 12,514 transactions were made, and the brokerage commissions produced total disaster. With an x value of 20 percent, only 110 transactions were made, and the strategy achieved an average annual return of 3.0 percent. If one had simply bought these same stocks and held them during this period, an average annual return of approximately 10.0 percent would have been realized. A number of other such formulas have been tested, sometimes over even longer periods of time, and strangely enough, there is little evidence to encourage us to believe that any of them would have been as productive as the simple buy-and-hold plan. Perhaps, if you find the random walk hypothesis appealing, this is not too surprising. Yet many of us find it hard to get over the idea that some such rule must be the key to better-than-average performance. The PhD's, however, seem to have decided that this is unlikely to be the case and are turning their computers to other tasks.

Advice

There is something very persuasive about the confident, confidential words of your broker on the phone, "I'm telling a few of my leading accounts to look very carefully at _____. Our research department in New York has been close to their management, and we have a very interesting set of developments coming up. I'm planning to pick up some for my own account. . . ." If you're willing to pay the price, you can get similar messages in telegrams from your advisory service which are delivered to your office just before the market opens. If you're paying for market advice, ask yourself a couple of questions, not so much about the quality of its market readings, but about its effect on you.

What is the actual effect of the advice on your behavior? Are you really using it, or just listening to it?

What is its effect on your moods, attitudes, and expectations?

Try out the following hypotheses on yourself. To what extent are they a useful mirror to show you the ways in which advice influences your financial operations?

A good deal of advice seems to consist of;

Company or industry data which is already known to market professionals and thus reflected in their actions before it comes to you,

A steady stream of buy recommendations, with almost never a sell recommendation.

Many sources of advice discuss stocks, the market, and the economy. Very, very few discuss you, your emotions, and your past failure and successes.

People willingly pay for advice which they seldom follow because it:

is highly entertaining,

gives a plausible interpretation of things that have already happened,

gives them a feeling of knowing what the real insiders, the smart money boys, are thinking,

is a powerful stimulant to fantasies of wealth, keeping alive the GRQ notion.

People do, on the other hand, sometimes follow advice because it;

relieves them of having to make some very difficult decisions,

stimulates their greed,

reduces their uncertainty,

reduces their anxiety and fear, builds their confidence.

People generally are quite willing to be told what to do with their money by a confident, authoritative sounding source which supplements advice with plausible arguments. These arguments are almost never examined critically or challenged.

Advisory services often advertise their short term track record if this happens to be favorable at the moment. They almost never reveal a long term track record. Their advertising strategies suggests that they depend heavily on the attraction of new subscribers in the late stages of a rising market. At such a point, they can exhibit a good recent track record, encounter a fresh wave of investor optimism about stocks, and find lots of people around who feel they have missed out on the rise which has already taken place. These people subscribe so as not to miss out on any more of the opportunities which "everybody else" has been enjoying. There is little, if any, data on subscription renewal rates to indicate what ultimately happens to these clients. Nor, for that matter, is there any public data on the rate at which people lose their fascination with their broker and make a change.

Such evidence as is available, suggests that advisory services, perhaps even the best brains in Wall Street may not do much better than the averages in the long run. If they are producing investment ideas which really appeal to their clients these opportunities are quickly wiped out of existence by the competitive bids of those trying to take advantage of them. From time to time studies appear which may serve to keep these doubts alive. Recently one examination of short term recommendations made by institutional brokers showed that only 47 percent of their suggestions outperformed the market in the following twelve months. If this is characteristic, their results are "pretty average."

In a recent Ford Foundation study, the ten year performance records of 36 college endowment funds were examined. Thirty-two of these did not do as well as the Standard and Poor's 500 stock index for the same period.

Advisory services make use of more or less subtle devices to appeal to our needs and emotions. There are several readily identifiable ways of engaging our attention.

To be bullish when the general trend appears to be down is a powerful stimulant to our tendencies toward wishful thinking.

To be bearish when everybody else sees a continued rise is to awaken our worst fears.

If there is a surprising drop in the market, everybody takes a beating. There is a tendency to forgive the advisory service as a companion in misery. Everybody is human, and in the same boat. To miss a rise, however, is far more serious, and not as likely to be forgiven.

A generally bullish tendency is thus a good policy for an advisory service.

To talk about "strong upside moves," "most rewarding commitments," and "outstanding appreciation possibilities" is to make a discreet attempt to awaken our latent GRQ desires.

There is the "stauch conservative" disclaimer that "we cannot, of course, guarantee the future effectiveness of our recommendations, but OH BOY, look what we've done in the past."

There are the obvious methods of trying to enhance credibility. "We have been in close touch with top management," or "based on our computerized, thirty variable, regression model, it would appear that. . . ."

Along with a recommendation which seems to run counter to the prevailing opinion, an attempt is often made to project the image of the fearless, courageous, independent thinker.

The point of raising these hypotheses is not to discount advice, but to see the effects it is actually having on us. If we were to consistently follow advice, many of us would surely do better in our financial operations than is presently the case. The question is whether we are just reading the interesting letters from the advisory service, or whether we are actually in there doing something about it. Many of us are not doing very well simply because we are not doing anything at all. It may well be your conclusion that expensive advice plays a stronger role in influencing your emotions than it does in influencing your actions.

It's Easy to Be About Average

Try to make some initial determinations as to what part research and advice might play in your GRS plan. My own conclusions might be ticked off about this way.

There is probably no approach yet available which seems to consistently yield better than average performance for a given level of risk.

It would be very expensive to undertake a serious search for an approach which would consistently yield better than average performance at a given level of risk. Not only expensive, but the probability of success is very low.

If better than average performance is difficult, average performance is easy, if only we do our part.

Average performance at a moderate level of risk may be quite good enough to get rich slowly.

A Different Kind of Research

If you take a broad look at research for the individual financial manager, the "small investor," there are at least two kinds of research to consider.

Stock market research in the usual sense, which we have been considering.

Research on our own behavior in financial operations, and the way the market influences our behavior.

Not much is ordinarily said about the latter kind of research. Contrary to the usual supposition, it may well be that this second kind of investigation can make a far bigger contribution to a GRS program than the first kind. The next problem to look at is how one might test this very odd hypothesis.

4

The Systems Approach

You and the market as an interactive system. Things the market does to you without your realizing it. Solving the "everybody makes money" puzzle. What to look for when you look at yourself. What character do you play? What's your style?

The Evidence

The most useful, yet most sadly neglected, data about the market is the data which tells us what happens to people when they actually put their money on the line. There are differences, interesting and useful differences, between:

Reading a book about the market and actually doing what it suggests.

Listening to "good, sound advice" and actually following it.

Firmly resolving to follow a financial plan and resisting the frequent and strong temptations to forget it.

Learning from simulated, make-believe market operations and learning from real operations involving one's own funds.

Knowing it's sensible to sell at highs and actually bringing one's self to do it when everybody else thinks there's no end in sight.

Planning to buy at lows and actually putting your money down when everyone is highly pessimistic about the market ever coming back.

Seeing the great logic of sometimes taking a loss and actually telling your broker to sell out a losing position.

Behaving like a pro and behaving like an amateur in your financial operations.

There are still other kinds of evidence around which can be very useful if we devote a little effort to making useful sense of it.

Successful brokers seem almost more interested in the emotions and attitudes of their customers than 'in the market itself.

In a recent study of 8,782 commodity speculators over a nine month period, it turned out that 75 percent of them showed a net loss.

The primary reason for this result was a reluctance to close out a losing position.

Psychologists have persistently shown that pressures, anxieties, tensions, and fears seriously degrade our skills as decision makers.

This evidence begins to make a little sense if we go at it from the viewpoint of modern systems analysis. To do this, we need to alter our usual level of observation. Instead of studying the market and trying to understand its almost infinitely complex behavior, we need to examine ourselves and the market as interacting components of a single system. Instead of exclusive trying to understand what we can do to the market, we need to add to our concern the things the market can do to us. To become sensitive to the effects the market may have on us and the ways these effects, in turn, influence our financial operations, is to see a system in which the parts act on and react to one another. This, our basic hypothesis, is likely to be far more helpful to our ultimate financial performance than exclusively studying the stock tables and earnings reports.

To act in this manner will require a degree of self-perception and self-awareness which is far from usual for most of us. It suggests that the really productive kind of research is not more testing of the random walk hypothesis. What is more likely to make a difference in one's financial operations is research on one's own plans, attitudes, and emotions. This, it begins to appear, may be the real secret of consistent financial effectiveness. It may be *the* essential prerequisite to getting rich slowly with a very high probability of success. It is almost surely the key to understanding why most people do not get rich at all.

Seeing yourself and the market as influencing each other is the real clue to getting the most out of your GRQ experiments. As interesting as you will find the progress of your commitments, what may be of even greater long term interest is your own progress through the GRQ experiment. As you look at your experiment and, indeed, as you look at all your financial operations, see if you can detect some of the ways the market is influencing you: For example:

How do you feel when you've experienced a sudden large loss or large gain? Does the emotional impact show up in the way you deal with your job, your family, or the next financial decision you make? Does it affect your attitude toward your family budget? Toward taking your spouse out for dinner? Toward the kids' next request?

Are the funds you're using all you have on which to retire, educate the children, or meet a major emergency? Does the fear and tension associated from the possibility of wiping out your financial future bring you to a high state of nervousness or panic when the market drops sharply?

Are you holding some things that went down a long time ago and stayed there, hoping that one of these days you'll be able to get even and get out?

Are you losing sleep over your financial operations? Are you a worrier? Do you call your broker frequently and read everything you can get your hands on, searching for fragments which tend to confirm your judgment and restore a little of your confidence?

Do you feel that you should be in the market all the time? Can you stay out for awhile, or are you too afraid of missing a rise?

Do you get upset by the stories of people who have made a killing?

When your holdings are up, everybody is feeling great, and stock market news begins to appear on the front page, do you decide that we're in for a whole new era of prosperity, that it's easy to make lots of money, that there's no end in sight, and that the best thing to do is hold and buy more?

When the market goes down and everyone is discouraged, do you avoid buying anything, promise yourself you'll quit the market forever if you can only get out even, and feel like a personal failure has occurred?

When you buy a stock, are you certain that it will go up? When it goes down, do you feel that you've made a mistake?

Do you honestly have a clear idea of what your past financial performance has been, or is there a lot there you really are not too interested in remembering?

Are there one or two really dramatic killings that you've made in the past which left you highly elated and which keep you trying again and again for that same great feeling?

Are you able to turn aside the advice, tips, and rumors which constantly come to your attention, or are you afraid of missing out on something really great?

Are you buying the current "market favorites" which are getting a lot of publicity, leading the market in volume at the moment, and have shown recent dramatic rises?

Are your decisions generally consistent with the overall trend of the market or are you operating against it?

Do you have a clear idea of your financial goals? How often do these seem to change? How do the movements of your portfolios influence your goals?

Have you tried out several systems or approaches to the market, had miserable results with each one, and moved on to another? Are you generally pretty discouraged·with the results of your past financial operations but persistently hopeful that you'll find a scheme for doing better?

Do you read most of the latest books on how to do dramatic things in the market? Do you enjoy what you read?

Do you study past performances of particular stocks, continually calculating how rich you'd be if you'd only bought them at the right moment, and then sold them at another right moment?

Do you have little love affairs with certain stocks, hanging on to them because you know them and they have done well for you in the past?

Is your program of financial operations kind of random, hit-or-miss, or "flexible"? Does it get a lot more of your attention when the market is going up than when it's going down?

Could you say that you have a systematic plan or approach to the market? Have you written it down? Could you say honestly that you've pretty well stuck to your plan for several years?

Does it seem that there are so many different kinds of opportunities available that you can hardly decide what to do? Do you often jump out of a recent commitment because something that seems better comes to your attention?

When you buy a stock, are you able to explicitly admit to yourself that there is some possibility that it won't do what you expect it to do?

When you make a commitment, do you have a written record of why, and what you expect it to do? Or do you regard this as unnecessary because you can easily remember all that?

Do you have some sources of information which you tend to use consistently? Or do you search more or less randomly through a great many different sources and types of information?

When things are going well, do you talk freely to others about your operations? When they are not going well, do you avoid the subject entirely?

This is more than enough to give you the idea. Try developing your own hypothesis about what the market may be doing to you. Once you get sensitive to the possibilities, you'll see yourself reacting in all sorts of interesting ways. Later on we'll talk about what to do about all this. I'm convinced that if your past financial operations have not been very satisfying, there may be some discoveries ahead for you which will make an interesting difference. For the moment, just try out the idea that the market does indeed do things to you, things which get reflected in your decision making behavior.

Resolving a Basic Dilemma

How is it that technicians seem to go right on making money in spite of the very persuasive random walk hypothesis? Why do the professionals tend to have so little concern for the work of the PhD's? Why aren't the PhD's getting richer? How come fundamentalists, contrarians, and astrological types all seem to make money if they are professionals? Why do so many of us pay for advice and not use it with any consistency? If professional advice is of very limited value, why do big institutions rely on it? Why do professionals seem to make money with such a great variety of different approaches to the market?

You may be of the opinion that professionals don't make much money and you may be right. I'm convinced, however, that generally speaking they make more than most of us and that none of them seems to have a consistently better approach in the long run than any of their colleagues. All of this strikes me as a kind of dilemma. It seems to say that what the professionals have is something besides their system, their approach, and their basic theories of the market. These are not simple questions and it is idle to suppose otherwise. Yet, some measure of understanding may emerge from a simply stated principle.

Getting deliberately rich or achieving consistent financial performance is at least as much a psychological problem as it is a logical problem.

The real function of a stock market system or theory is to lead us toward a set of more or less reasonable operating rules which will protect us from ourselves. Left alone to suffer all the emotional impacts of the market on our decision making abilities, we are almost sure to do things which are self-defeating. We hang on too long to a losing position, rush almost blindly into risky speculations, change our objectives frequently, get greedy and try for more and more, or get discouraged and give up. Left alone, we seem prone to decisions which we later come to regret, because when our emotions subside we can see that they didn't make much sense as a consistent and sensible approach to the market. This contrariness of emotional behavior, its inconsistency with good market performance, seems to me to be the top candidate for explaining why "the small investor always gets taken." The function which can be served by almost any reasonable set of operating rules is to keep us insulated from the psychological pressures which the market generates. These psychological pressures seem to have the peculiar effect of making us do things which can only result in a very low level of market performance. The unaided investor, the investor without some consistent approach, just doesn't seem to have a long run chance.

Here, it seems to me, we are very close to understanding how there can be professionals who get consistent performance with many different approaches to the market. There are in fact many different market theories which can perform *the* essential function of supporting and encouraging systematic, unemotional financial operations. An approach to the market may be technical, fundamental, or involve almost any reasonably coherent set of ideas. It need not be complex, subtle, or novel. It simply needs to make some minimal degree of sense to the person using it, and it has to be *followed*. In this sense there seem to be lots of good approaches and probably very, very few outstanding ones. Some may be a little better than others at forecasting the movements of the market, but many of them seem able to perform the function of insulating us from our own emotional natures, of helping us avoid our naturally counterproductive market behavior.

It is even possible, and perhaps quite common among professionals, to achieve good performance with an underlying theory of the market which gives a wrong indication of price movements more often than not. In the hands of a professional, who actually has the poise to apply the grand old trading approach of "cut your losses and let your profits run," it is perfectly possible to evolve a system on which the underlying theory is wrong 60 percent of the time, but the profits which are actually realized the other 40 percent of the time more than make up for the losses. The missing ingredient for most of us is the actual ability, the poise, the calm detachment, to cut our losses and let our profits run.

Almost any reasonable approach is better than the random, emotionally determined behavior that is likely to result from no approach at all. Even a simple "buy and hold" plan is probably better than the self-defeating behavior which is likely to follow from an unplanned surrender to our needs, drives, and emotions.

One doesn't want to stick blindly to his plan no matter what happens. On the whole, however, it is probably better to stick with it than dump it, even in the face of quite a high degree of doubt. A lot of approaches seem capable of giving a long run average performance which is better than that achieved by those who seem to be shifting frequently from one approach to another. One of the best courses is to decide in advance the conditions under which one should change his approach, and make this a part of the plan. If you change, do it deliberately, not emotionally. Otherwise, there seems to be a considerable likelihood that whims, chance rumors, and attempts to rationalize losses will distract you from the original logic of your ideas. Even better is to build into your strategy a way of getting to a relatively safe or liquid position when all of your expectations seem to have gone wrong. This not only gives you the chance to recover, but enhances your poise and prevents fear from dominating reason.

Self-Awareness

To look at ourselves as components of a system in which we do things in the market and it does things to us is to focus on the real difficulty of the GRS hypothesis. It is probably relatively easy to design a simple GRS program which, *if followed*, has a very high probability

of making one rich. The probability of following a plan over the necessarily extended period of time is unhappily quite small for most of us.
It is significantly more important to devote our energies to increasing
this probability, than to devote them to learning more about the market.
There is a greater return from efforts aimed at understanding our own
lack of poise, our own impatience, our own emotionally tainted thinking, than there is from an equal effort devoted to reading research reports from one's broker.

The thing which most distinguishes the amateur from the professional in financial operations is, simply, self-awareness. The secret of the
professional, I'm now convinced, is the discovery that they can dramatically increase their chances of success by watching themselves even
more carefully than they watch the market. The thing about the pros
is not so much the specific knowledge of investment opportunities they
have, but the fact that they know enough about themselves to protect
themselves from themselves.

In the Looking Glass

The way to watch one's self is to look in a mirror, a mirror of whatever sort to catch the kind of reflection one wants. Psychiatrists are high
priced mirrors that provide reflections in depth. Perhaps, however, something useful can be achieved with a far less expensive, do-it-yourself
kind of reflection process. Perhaps you will find fascination in three
useful types of looks at yourself.

What is your self-image as a financial manager?

What is your personal style as a decision maker?

In what specific ways do you and the market interact as a system?

The first two possibilities we will look into immediately. The third
will require the next several chapters for a useful discussion. There we
suggest what you may find to be some revealing experiments to help you
learn about the system of financial operations in which you play only
one part.

Seeing Yourself in the System

Looking at ourselves as part of a system rests for its effectiveness on
the idea that once we understand something of the forces which shape
our thought and behavior we are in a position to influence ourselves.
We will have some chance of disengaging ourselves from our inner

conflicts, distortions, and frustrations, and thus take greater control of our decision making. To the extent we become aware of the unconscious drives from within, we can perhaps learn to deal with them and thus expand our power over our behavior. The more fully the origins of behavior are understood, the greater our freedom from compulsion. More satisfying decisions will come, not only from the usual feedback of experience, but also from the study of one's inhibitions and repressions.

We should, however, probably be alerted by a caution which comes from counsellors and therapists who are working to understand the behavior of others. While self-analysis is, by its very nature, a matter of consciousness, explicitness, and deliberation, change need not be. It turns out to be important to understand behavior as a basis for change which may take place quite naturally. Change need not be a matter of careful calculation, deliberate decision aids, or explicit efforts to make different sorts of decisions. Given understanding, change will follow without effort or forcing.

Not all of us, however, will have the patience or the conviction that this would seem to require. Some of our discussion will concern quite explicit and rather definite plans for modifying our behavior. Perhaps this will be useful, but perhaps we should not take it too seriously. It seems to be very important to work hard at understanding, but not as important to work hard at changing. Make a real effort to become aware of your style and the things which shape it, but go easy, relax, do not become compulsive about trying to alter it. Change may somehow be so intimately connected with understanding that the two will occur almost together. Perhaps what we most need is patience, since it may be possible to try too hard. There may be a danger in too much striving. The danger is suggested by what is known as the "law of reversed effect."

This law suggests that if we are too eager to diagnose ourselves and lay out a program of change, our chances of being effective are considerably reduced. The greater our eagerness, the longer it will take. Success will come more quickly to those who try to understand without an impatience to make changes. "To give in is to overcome, to be humble is to succeed." The best approach is to work for clear self-awareness without interfering too much. It is more important to see and understand what one is doing, than to strive for improvements. Grim determination doesn't appear to be the best recipe for change.

We are sometimes agreeably surprised to notice that changes have taken place in our deciding without any very deliberate effort at all. Perhaps they reflect some suggestion once briefly considered but quickly forgotten or someone we had quite casually watched in action. Our understanding of ourselves probably ought to extend to the possibility of too much exertion for changes and of expecting too much from any good intentions we might develop.

Your Self-Image

First try to give a general characterization of yourself as you behave in your financial management capacities. How would you broadly describe the way in which you and the market interact? Can you, for example, cast yourself comfortably in one of the roles which follow, or do you need to create a special characterization to really capture your special individuality?

The Investor — with a capital "I," conservative, in blue chips only, long holding periods, interested mostly in fundamentals, thinks speculation is bad, proud of an ability to ignore short term market fluctuations, aiming at distant goals.

The Trader — in and out, lots of phone calls, right up on latest market developments, hopes for short, sharp profits, not much interested in fundamentals or even in what business the company is in, watches the tape whenever possible, spends lunch hours in his broker's office.

The Big Operator — has lunch at expensive places with his broker, barks snappy buy and sell orders over the office phone in the midst of regular business activities, gives tips voluntarily, loves to be asked for advice, has endless stories of past triumphs, always has *Wall Street Journal* on his desk.

The Surprise Millionaire — admires the stories of the little old ladies who went around for years in ragged clothes and were later found to have made vast amounts in the market and outsmarted all the big men on Wall Street, expects to find a sure-fire system one day soon, will emerge eventually and show everybody when he's piled it up.

The Philanthropist — fantasies of a Ford Foundation with his name on it, scientists will cure cancer with his money, politicians will save the country with his money, and little people in trouble everywhere will be eternally grateful for his help.

The Big Talker — favorite (and only) topic of conversation is the market and his past killings, generally not very successful but always in possession of some inside information which he is willing to share, expresses strongly derogatory opinions about brokers, banks, institutions, and the government.

Stars and Stripes — buys government bonds on the payroll savings plan, is emotionally patriotic about it, regards them as the only safe investment, frequently asserts that if our government isn't secure, nothing is.

Inflation Fighter — feels the continual hot pursuit of rising prices, thinks this is both inevitable and the road to ultimate destruction of our society, continually bemoans the latest price increase which he has experienced, puts every penny in common stocks as a hedge against inflation, doesn't really know how this is working out.

The SAP Man — puts money regularly and religiously into a mutual fund systematic accumulation program which a salesman got him into a few years ago, doesn't know how his fund is doing in relation to others, feels trapped, locked in by front end load charges.

Book Buyer — has read a good many of the hundreds of books available about the market, enjoys them immensely, resolves firmly after reading each one to do exactly what it says as soon as he recovers from doing what the last one said, doesn't do much of anything, but relies on reading for constant stimulation of his fantasies.

The Accumulator-Plunger — accumulates cash in his checking account, the more cash he piles up, the more he forgets about his past market disasters and the more vulnerable he becomes to the next GRQ opportunity to come his way, plunges, then swears off the market forever and repeats the cycle.

The Diverse Investor

You can build your own characterization of yourself and you may enjoy doing it. Try not to make a judgment about the goodness or ineffectiveness of any of those I've outlined above or of your own work. Just think of these as dispassionate summaries of the data about your behavior. Don't be too hard on yourself, but don't distort what is there when you take a hard-nosed look at yourself. This is very likely to be a useful first step toward a professional degree of self-awareness. Try the experiment on pages 123–127.

Some Dimensions of Personal Style

Now take a little more precise look at your behavior, this time at the way you make decisions. How do you look as a decision maker? What is your personal style of deciding? Try yourself out on the following dimensions of personal style. See page 122.

To what extent is your style of decision making intuitive, implicit, and private? To what extent is it analytical, explicit, and open?

To what degree are you tolerant of ambiguity in a decision situation? Can you decide in the face of ambiguous notions about objectives or ambiguous statements of the alternative courses of action? Some studies suggest that experienced decision makers are highly tolerant of ambiguity and capable of resolving it in their own special ways.

Similarly, to what degree are you tolerant of uncertainty as to the consequences of various actions? Some of us require considerable information and assurance before we will act, others are far more willing to act on the basis of limited information and substantial uncertainty. We should not imagine that one such style is always "better" than the other.

How reasonable is your hindsight? How effectively do you learn from your past decisions? Are you given to regretting decisions which turn out badly or do you suppress these feelings and look to the future? Do you distinguish clearly between a good decision which depends on reason and logic, and a good result or outcome which always depends to some degree on chance, luck, and circumstances beyond your control?

How much cognitive effort do you invest in a decision? Some decision makers are careful and deliberate thinkers, others tend to proceed "off the top of their heads" or "by the seat of their pants."

To what degree do you seek external aids or outside help in deciding?

To what extent is there a need for coherence between your beliefs, your actions, and your objectives?

We may seek coherence by becoming more optimistic about a course of action after we have chosen it, than before. Sometimes we adopt the belief that what we have become committed to is the best possible course of action, while we had no such conviction prior to our commitment. We achieve coherence or reduce "cognitive dissonance" by revising our perceptions.

How sensitive are your unaided decision making abilities to conditions of stress? There is considerable evidence that most of us become distinctly poorer decision makers when we are under stress or pressure.

To what extent are your perceptions and thoughts influenced, not so much by the external world, as by our own needs and desires. One of the great discoveries of modern psychology is that what we see and what we think are influenced subconsciously by our needs and tensions.

To what degree are you clear about your own decision making processes? How much self-knowledge or self-consciousness do you have in this connection? It is well established that we seldom understand very well the reasons we do what we do, or the goals we are striving to attain.

To what degree are your perceptions of the external world distorted because of distortions shared by your associates? Science is full of instances of socially shared distortions, often going about under the heading of "common sense." Indeed, one of the best definitions of common sense pictures it as that kind of sense which tells us when we look out of the window that the world is flat.

To what degree do you abstract or simplify the external world in making a decision?

To what degree do you rely on rules of thumb or platitudes for disposing of decision problems?

To what degree do you look ahead in a decision? Is the planning horizon in the relatively near, or relatively distant future? One of the skills of a good chess player is his ability to look ahead to the future consequences of his moves. The ability of computers to play chess is rather directly related to their "look-ahead" ability.

When things are looking very bad, how good are you at remaining calm and free from a slight panicky feeling?

How much experience do you have in living with the consequences of your choices? Have you made some "big" decisions?

How strong is your desire to get immediate, remarkable results when you make a decision?

What can you say about your ability to see the facts, the data, both sides of a question, when you are confronted with an emotionally charged decision situation?

How do you rate yourself in terms of self-confidence and respect for your own abilities?

How capable are you of filtering through and giving structure to large volumes of information?

Do you have a tendency to write down important considerations when you have to make a decision of some consequence?

There is little use in trying to decide in advance whether one style of deciding is "better" than another. It's foolish to suppose that anyone could give you a set of rules for making financial decisions which you would actually follow. Something of greater subtlety, but also of greater practicality is involved. Only you yourself can (and should) make useful judgments about the quality and effectiveness of your financial decision making. Only if you make these judgments, will actual behavioral changes result. You've got to begin by appreciating your own self-image, by seeing your own style, and by becoming conscious of what you ordinarily do without the slightest self-consciousness. Then compensation and change will begin to occur, almost entirely without effort on your part.

In the next several chapters we will get down to the specifics, trying to suggest some useful things you might undertake to find out about yourself as you interact with the market; things which have a good change of making your success with a GRS program more likely.

Keep in Mind This Hypothesis

The function of a system or approach is not to produce astounding performance, but rather to guide us into actually executing our financial operations in some reasonably consistent manner. The great contribution of an approach or system is to keep us operating according to some more or less plausible set of theories and principles. It serves to keep us both from doing nothing and from making some deliberately foolish moves. In this sense, there may not be any great systems, but there are probably a very large number of good ones.

What the professional money managers have that we do not may simply be that they are in there doing something and that they act in accordance with some reasonable set of ideas about the market. They may be technicians, fundamentalists, or whatever. By being in there in a consistent fashion they achieve average results. Many of us don't do that.

This is why most systems enjoy some measure of long run success *if they are actually followed*. In the short run, they will sometimes look better than average and sometimes worse. People who decide to try out a system after it has just shown a period of better than average performance, then get discouraged and give it up after a period of worse than average performance, will naturally show very poor long run results.

Do Something

The important thing for a GRS program is to be in there doing something. Not necessarily fully invested all the time, but paying attention and operating according to some methodical approach, not by random responses to unchecked emotions. Most people don't do anything with any degree of consistency. Some spend their time looking for a GRS system and end up doing nothing. A lot of us would be far better off if we picked a reasonable approach and actually used it. In the long run we'd achieve about average results for the level of risk we chose. We'd be a lot richer than those who sat on their hands. Not very many people would be better off than us. The message seems to be to me, "Quit looking for a way to get exceptional performance. Get in there and get average performance."

5

How to be
a Cost-Effective
Information Processor

*Which is worse, too little information or too much?
Applying a basic principle for determining what is a
reasonable amount of information to accumulate before deciding. The snap decision maker and the super-
informed investor. A little cost-effectiveness analysis
of your information processing behavior. Developing
a strategy for beating the market.*

Your Money's Worth

Ask someone what will most help him in improving his investment results. He will very likely say, "More information." It rather seldom occurs to people that their problems might arise from devoting too much
time and money to gathering information, getting swamped with more
information than they can reasonably make use of, or not making very
effective use of the information they already have available. A rather reliable human characteristic is that when we think about making better
decisions, we think about getting more "facts" or data. We rarely find
ourselves thinking about giving more structure to the decision situation.
Almost every book on the stock market contains some version of the

prudent warning against buying on the basis of too little information. The person who buys a stock without even finding out what the company makes is usually singled out as the shocking extreme of not properly investigating a commitment. The person who makes commitments on the basis of too little information is, however, more likely to attain his objectives than those of us who get so mired in data that we never buy anything at all. Clearly there is a problem of too little information and a problem of too much information.

A very important question is, "How much information is it reasonable to collect before making a decision?" The answer is very largely connected with the sort of information you're collecting and how you're processing that information in your decision making. Here is a very precise sounding guiding principle which is highly rational.

Go on collecting more and more information until the expected cost of collecting the next increment of information exceeds the expected value or gain you are likely to realize from it.

That is, as long as getting additional information looks like it will be worth more than it costs, go ahead. If additional information looks like it will cost more than it's worth, stop.

No one seriously believes that this principle can be applied with great precision to financial operations. It is almost impossible for most of us to give a satisfying answer to the question of what cost should be ascribed to the time we spend in the evening reading about the stock market and about various investment opportunities.

Likewise, it is extraordinarily difficult to say much about the value of some information we have not yet obtained. (Yet we do this implicitly whenever we agree to pay for information or advice, or even decide to devote our own efforts to obtaining it.) Still, it turns out to be very useful indeed for many of us to think about this principle, and make some rough and ready assessments of our own information processing behavior with it.

One way to achieve consistently superior financial results is to be able to regularly obtain "inside" information. If you can be among the very first to know and act on information about earnings, new products, discoveries, buying and selling intentions, and so on; if you have a way of regularly (and legally) being on the inside, then you wouldn't be reading this book. If you are reading this book, forget about the real inside information. By the time you and I find out about these things, the insiders have already had plenty of opportunity to act on them. Unless we make a very different assessment of the information than they do, it tends to be pretty much valueless by the time we read about it. There is a relentless law about the value of information:

if it's consistently free, it's consistently worthless.

There are those of us who buy whatever our broker or our brother-in-law makes a strong pitch for, spending little or no time getting much of any information. While it is probably unwise to advocate this approach (unless you have a very special brother-in-law), it may not be unreasonable to raise a couple of questions before disposing of such advice.

If this leads to unsatisfactory results, how much of the difficulty could be ascribed to lack of reasonably available information? Not information that would have required some supernatural clairvoyance, but information that might realistically have been available at the time the decision was made.

If this type of investor has below average results, how much of the problem can be attributed to the original commitment and how much to the way it was subsequently managed? Was the commitment held after it had reached its original profit objective, only to see it suddenly retreat and be sold at a lower level? Did what began as a short term possibility of gain actually result in the holding of a long term losing position?

Whatever the case against the snap decision maker, he is not really helped by those wise counsellors who appeal to the conventional logic by urging that we get *all* the facts before investing. The snap decision maker is at least in the market. You can't win if you don't play. Surely there will be times when he will realize that if he had only gotten a little more information, he would have made a different and more profitable decision. If he *thinks* about this, he will gradually adjust his view of the cost and value of additional data and approach a more reasonable information processing strategy.

Too Much Data

At the other extreme from the snap judgment man is the super-informed investor who handles lots and lots of data. The *Wall Street Journal* every weekday, a couple of research reports from his broker in the evening, at least one expensive advisory service, and all sorts of company reports. In his most unhappy form, the super-informed investor spends so much time poring through his vast information supply that he hardly ever feels well enough informed to make a commitment. On the one hand he is intolerant of ambiguity, fearful of "making a mistake," and thoughtless of the value of his own time. On the other hand, he harbors the feeling that if he keeps on looking he'll come across a "sure thing," some piece of information which will resolve all his uncertainty and show him an almost certain opportunity for profit. Almost pathologically, he persists, because he cannot make himself go ahead when there seems to be so much information that he hasn't yet explored. To be super-informed is clearly to spend more time and money on information processing than the returns are likely to justify. Most of us would like to achieve a position of moderation between those who leap without much looking and those who drown themselves in the attempt to get "all the facts and figures."

It is naive to suppose that we can readily balance in our minds the costs and benefits of our data collection and opportunity seeking efforts. Yet the roughest judgments about these costs and benefits will surely suffice to show us whether we are at one extreme or the other. It seems very likely that most of us can achieve more satisfying decisions if we simply wonder from time to time, where we stand with respect to costs, in both time and money, of our efforts and the benefits we seem to be deriving. Even the first steps toward self-awareness may be rewarding here.

A Little Cost-Effectiveness Analysis

Once we get the notion that persistent searching is not likely to yield a sure thing, some very rough order-of-magnitude calculations can perform the useful function of getting us a little closer to the right ball park. Don't take these calculations too seriously. They may, however, have a certain arresting effect if your behavior seems wildly at variance with them.

What value to place on your own time? This is always a very difficult question to answer comfortably. If you are actually giving up the opportunity to earn x dollars per hour when you devote yourself to your financial planning, then x dollars is a good figure to use. The difficulty is that most of us do our planning in our "free" time or leisure time when regular employment is not available. For many of us "moonlighting" is not a realistic alternative that we seriously consider. Still what we regularly earn provides a place to start. If your job brings you $5, $10, or $20 per hour, it might be helpful to at least ask yourself if your free time is worth half as much or twice as much to you.

If you value your time at $10 per hour and if you think that you can almost certainly improve your investment results from 10 percent to 20 percent annual return, then it would make some sense to put in about ten hours per year for each $1,000 you manage. If you think you can raise the average level of your performance from 10 percent to 30 percent, then it would be roughly reasonable to put in 20 hours per year for each $1,000. Recognize, however, that this makes sense only if you are pretty certain of success, and that for most of us the chances of raising our performance from 10 percent to 30 percent are rather small.

Table 5-1

Planning Hours Per Year Per $1000

Performance Improvement	Value of Your Time		
	$5.00 per hour	$10.00 per hour	$20.00 per hour
5 percent	10 hours	5 hours	2.5 hours
10	20	10	5
15	30	15	7.5
20	40	20	10

In Table 5-1 we have exhibited these simple kinds of calculations. What remains to be done, is to add your view of the chances of success in making the indicated gain in performance. Again, don't take these numbers too seriously but see if they don't lead you to some interesting rough judgments about the cost-effectiveness of your financial planning efforts.

If you are interested in doing all your planning in one lump now and nothing further in the future, then you need to make some sort of judgment about the length of time over which this planning will extend. Two years, five years, or even more. This will lead you to make some obvious adjustments in the table.

If you place no value at all on your leisure time, then you probably ought to devote every available moment to financial planning, as long as there seems to be any chance at all of improving your performance. Put this way, most of us conclude that we do indeed implicitly place some non-zero value on our free time.

Including Uncertainty

It's perfectly possible to go even further if one gets interested in being a little bit explicit about the uncertainty which surrounds investment opportunities. If, for example, we were looking at a number of possibilities, it would be reasonable to say that the more uncertain we are about a particular opportunity, the more information we ought to seek about it. We should value information according to its effect in reducing our uncertainty. The more it reduces this uncertainty, the more valuable it is. We say information is irrelevant or valueless when it has no effect on our uncertainty. It is useful in this connection, to make an attempt to be roughly explicit about the level of uncertainty that we are willing to tolerate. The more costly and difficult it is to get uncertainty reducing information, the more uncertainty it would be reasonable to tolerate. It is *never* reasonable to try to get *all* the facts. Applied roughly as they must be, these notions may have some effect in preventing us from behaving in ways which we might later reflect on as highly unreasonable.

Similarly, the problem of how much effort to expend searching for a "good deal" or a better deal can be usefully illuminated by means of a little explicitness. Most of us would like to be somewhere between grabbing the first thing which comes to our attention and an endless search process in which we find ourselves always holding off in anticipation of something better which is yet to emerge. While search goes on, one is not only spending time and money, but perhaps giving up profits. Search is thus clearly not free. The better the best of your presently available opportunities are, the smaller the probability that additional search effort will produce any improvement. Put another way, the better the options you now have, the smaller the chances you'll be pleased with the results of further search. All this has an obvious common sense ring to it. It seems likely, however, that the uncommonness of common sense is an enduring truth. It may sound to you like "what you would naturally do anyway," but take another look at yourself in the mirror.

What Information?

I'm not going to tell you exactly what information to collect or how to use it in your planning and decision making. Only if you do that for yourself, will much of anything actually happen in your financial operations. You can probably do a far better job than I anyway. By the time you get through this book, you'll have most of my ideas on what information is relevant and how it should be used, but do your best to ignore these notions. It may not be very hard. Your strategy must be your own creation if you are actually going to use it. If it's mine or somebody else's, you're unlikely to apply it, or do much more than glance at it. I do, however, urge on you the following preachment. Write. Write it all down. Write down a check list of the information you really want and will actually use on any stock you consider. For example:

Dividends for the last five years

Annual growth rate of earnings and sales

Closing prices daily for the last x months

Volume of trading for the last y months

Size of the company

Products and markets

Whatever you really want and can use

Recognize that a lot of the information you use only in the sense of checking to see if it falls in some region of acceptability. Other information helps you become explicit about your expectations for a stock and the uncertainty you associate with these expectations. Write out the list, but do more. Be as explicit as you possibly can about how you're really going to use the information. Why do you want the data on trading volume? How does this information actually get used in formulating your anticipations for the stock? You may very well discover that a lot of data doesn't have any explicit use which you are able to describe to yourself. You just want dividends or price-earnings ratios because everybody seems to want that information. Your own approach may not really have a place for these numbers. All of this reflection will be difficult and time consuming. It may, however, be very rewarding in terms of the cost-effectiveness of your information processing efforts. Chances are you'll discover that there is a lot of information you really don't need and some that you would really like to add to your check list.

Strategy Development

The check list and the specification of what you'll really do with the items on it are obviously the first step toward being explicit about your plan of financial operations or strategy. Here again a little rough and ready cost-effectiveness analysis may be both revealing and helpful.

Start with a simple strategy like those widely used by many of us:

Buy and hold a mutual fund.

Buy and hold your own portfolio of blue chips.

Buy x dollars worth of IBM every month—dollar cost averaging.

Now think about the possibilities for developing more complex strategies. How much effort would be required to achieve what kinds of chances of what sorts of performance improvements? There are people around (surely not you or me) who are working very hard to develop a system to "beat the market." If this means getting rich quick or annual gains which are consistently in the region of 50 percent or 100 percent, then I believe their chances of success are very small indeed. Efforts of this sort don't seem to me to be cost-effective, but you need to form your own conclusion.

Perhaps you will want to take a look again at some of the data in Chapter 3. The chances of developing a complex trading strategy which will yield consistently better than average performance at a given level of risk seem rather small to me. The chances of uncovering a superior approach to the market through fundamentals, through contrary opinion analysis, or through astrology seem to be quite small also. Once again, however, you need to work out these judgments for yourself. You are unique.

My own conclusions about being cost-effective in information processing are quite simple. The chances of finding an exceptional approach to the market are small but the chances of finding a good one are quite large. The important thing is to have some coherent plan for gathering information, forming anticipations, and then actually making your financial decisions. Have some coherent plan and use it. Use it through thick and thin. Random, helter-skelter information processing and decision making has a low probability of making one anything but broke. Even buying and holding blue chips has a fine chance of success if you can actually stick with it. Begin by writing down your plans for gathering data and making decisions. A recent study by the Mercantile Exchange revealed that brokers see the most common mistake among commodity traders to be failing to stick with their plans, or failing to have any plans at all. Many traders seem to go bust trying to ride the action to a peak.

6

Building
Your Track Record

*The basic idea behind the significant importance of
your track record. Designing your own prediction
and decision accounting system. What to record and
how to analyze it. The key behaviors to look for as
you interact with the market. Making a system flow
diagram.*

The Track Record Hypothesis

If you've designed and executed your GRQ experiment along the
lines outlined in Chapter 2, you may already have some appreciation
of the crucial importance of the written record in your research notebook. It is now a useful time to make a further test of the interesting
hypothesis that effort devoted to recording and understanding one's own
behavior will bring a greater increase in the chances of getting rich
than will effort devoted to recording and analyzing historical market
data. Hindsight won't get back the money you may have lost, but it may
do some things for you which are even more important. One of the most
valuable products of your financial operations may be information about

the ways in which you and the market interact. This sort of output is usually wasted because for many people its importance is quite unsuspected.

The essence of your track record is a written reflection of not only how your commitments turned out, but also how you made the predictions and decisions which led you into these commitments. It is a curious feature of conventional accounting systems of the business world that they keep the most careful track of the costs and revenues that result from management decisions, but keep no track at all of the decisions themselves. No firm has anything like an objective, dispassionate record of how the major decisions which influence its destiny were made. It would seem that the key to really learning something important from an accounting system would be to progress from simply accounting for outcomes and results to accounting for the decisions themselves.

Design

Your track record will only be really useful if it includes your own decision accounting system. Keeping track of your decisions need not be subtle or complicated, but it is too important to be done casually on the back of used envelopes. Make the kind of commitment to it that will keep you interested and will help keep you organized. If you have a research notebook in which your GRQ results are recorded, use it. Perhaps you will want to design some forms, very simple ones, to provide an orderly way of accumulating data on the hypothesis you wish to study about your predictions, your decisions, and how things actually turned out. Check lists are fine, or, if you don't like to write, dictate your observations into your tape recorder. Do a complete and careful job of labelling the tapes so you will be able to work with them easily. The three basic rules for building a track record are:

1/ Design your own. It must be yours and nobody else's.

2/ Keep it simple and easy to work with.

3/ Whatever happens, stick with it. It will grow progressively more valuable as a financial management tool.

Prediction Data

There will be several important kinds of data in your track record, among the most important of which will probably be the information which will enable you to study yourself as a predictor. Suppose, for example, that you are making a prediction, by whatever means seem reasonable to you, that a stock will go up ten points in the next year. Refine your prediction a little bit. What is the most likely gain, the most probable gain, the expected gain, or the gain that is about as likely to be exceeded as not to be reached? Maybe the answer to these questions is a gain of 10 points. Now ask yourslf what gain has only a 10 percent chance of being exceeded. Or 20 percent, or 5 or 1 percent. Whatever is comfortable for you to think about.

Suppose you take the view that there is only a 10 percent chance of the gain exceeding 20 points. You are 90 percent sure that the gain will not exceed 20 points, or you feel that there is only one chance in ten of a gain greater than 20 points. Make the same sort of judgment for the low side. What gain has only a 10 percent chance of not being achieved, a 90 percent chance of being exceeded? Maybe the answer you give yourself is not a gain at all, but a loss of 5 points. Your prediction could then be put in the form, "I'm 80 percent certain that in the next year this stock will not lose more than 5 points nor gain more than 20. My best guess, most probable value, or expected gain, is 10 points."

If this seems difficult at first, remember some of our discussion in Chapter 1. The habit, the style, of being explicit about one's uncertainty is not natural and takes some practice. You'll find, if you're like many people who have learned to do it, that being explicit grows rapidly easier and more interesting as you work at this practice.

The Reasons Why

Along with your prediction and the uncertainty associated with it, get down in your track record one or two leading reasons which lie behind your conclusion. Just a few words about the reasoning that led you to the prediction. This will be difficult at first because you will "just have a feeling" or work on the basis of "the seat of your pants," or what somebody told you. As your track record develops, you may be surprised to find it growing easier to be clear about why you make the prediction you do. To begin with, don't try for a long complex explanation, but just jot down one or two leading considerations that entered your thinking. An unexpected increase in earnings, a growing market, a new product, a strong management change, whatever played a role in your thinking.

You may be making predictions about next week, next month, or several years hence, but get them all down in your records. Obviously the nearer your planning horizon, the faster you'll accumulate data, but take the long view and write down even your longest term predictions. When the time actually rolls around, record what happened. Compare your prediction with what actually occurred. This is such a simple and useful thing to do that it is difficult to understand why so few people and so few businesses have made it a routine procedure.

Analysis

Each time you get an actual outcome it may be compared with your prediction at two interesting levels. First, simply compare the result with your expression of uncertainty when you made the prediction. If the actual gain for the stock turned out to be close to your expected gain, your most probable value, that's fine. You are either lucky or skillful, something which remains to be determined. If the actual gain falls outside the upper or lower 10 percent probability values, you may want to ask why. What did you fail to consider? What did you leave out? To what did you attribute too much importance? What was your market position at the time you made the prediction? What had been your immediate past history of gains and losses? What was your mood at the time? Is there any obvious way you could have improved the prediction?

If you're wondering at this point how to decide whether the actual outcome was "close" or "not so close" to your most probable value of expected value, you're getting the idea. Go ahead and refine this way of looking at yourself, making it more precise, more discriminating. Again, I can't give you any rules, your own design will be by far the best. You may wish to say that after you've made a prediction, if the result turns out to be inside your upper and lower x percent limits, you'll be satisfied. The difference between the outcome and your best guess or most probable value can be marked down to a myriad of small causes which is just too complex to sort out. If, however, the result falls outside the x percent probability limits then it might be worthwhile looking for an explanation. Can the miss be explained by looking at your own behavior or at market forces of some sort? If you set wide limits, you will be accepting some wide variations between predicted and actual values without further investigation. On the other hand, you won't be using a lot of your time trying to track down the causes of the variations; causes, which in some cases will be difficult to find and in all cases will be matters of some uncertainty themselves. If you set narrow limits, you will spend a much greater portion of your time looking for causes, but you will be likely to refine your predictions somewhat more quickly. You need to make your own judgments about these limits. There are no fixed rules.

When you've accumulated a modest amount of data on predictions and actual outcomes, say ten or more sets of observations, you can take a different kind of look at yourself. If the outcomes have a tendency to be consistently above your most probable value or consistently below it, then you may have an optimistic or pessimistic bias. You may, with some regularity, expect stocks to gain more than they do, or lose more than they do. Just knowing about this bias will usually be enough to help you correct it. This turns out to be one of the easiest kinds of improvements to make in your predicting behavior.

Studying Your Uncertainty

If the actual outcomes seem to fall outside your 10 percent probability limits with some regularity, you may feel a need to revise the uncertainty associated with your predictions. You might conclude that you are more certain than seems reasonable about your predictions, that you should acknowledge greater uncertainty, and that things are not quite as well behaved and dependable as you had thought. Similarly, if all of the outcomes tend to be tightly grouped within a range smaller than the range spanned by the 10 percent probability limits, you may find that you have been more uncertain than is warranted by the situation. Things are more dependable, more predictable, less uncertain than you had originally supposed.

A high degree of mathematical refinement is possible here, both in setting some limits and revising one's expressions of uncertainty, but such refinement may not be particularly cost-effective. You may want to test the hypothesis which I have come to believe, that the really big improvements can come from some very rough-and-ready track record studies.

As time permits, make some deliberate experiments with new and different methods of prediction. Take a look again at some of the ideas in Chapter 2 and make these experiments as productive as possible. Test out your advisory service, your broker, and your wife's (husband's) hunches. Develop your own explicit system, extrapolate the 200-day moving average, draw a straight line through the last x closing prices, or try whatever prediction system seems interesting.

Decision Accounting

Beyond your predictions, your track record needs to begin to accumulate your own decision accounting data. Think of a decision as occurring each time you make a deliberate commitment to buy or not to buy something. Keep track of what you decided to do, what you expected to happen, and the one or two most important considerations that led you to the conclusion. Just what to record about each decision is a very personal thing that you need to work out especially to suit yourself. As you learn some things about yourself, the sort of new questions you will want to study and the data you will record will change. You might wish, however, to start off with some of the items on the following list:

What alternative course of action were you considering?

What predictions did you make for each alternative course of action?

What were the major sources of uncertainty associated with each?

What future events seem most likely to influence your results?

Where did you get the idea for each course of action?

What sources of information did you use in making the predictions?

How much time had you spent searching for alternatives?

Who had you talked to in the period just prior to the decision?

How long had you thought about the decision?

Could you have justified the decision to your spouse? to your broker?

How had you been doing relative to the market as a whole prior to making the decision?

How had other people been doing?

What was the profit position of your portfolio at the time of the decision?

How much cash were you holding at the time of the decision?

Had there been a drastic change in your market outlook just prior to the decision?

How had things been going at work? with the family?

How had you been feeling, both physically and mentally?

What had you been doing just before deciding?

Could you have waited a little while without losing the opportunities?

Is the decision consistent with your GRS program?

What To Look For

I could produce a very long list indeed, but you need to work this out for yourself. The really useful results of your track record experiments can be some insights into the conditions under which your own decision making abilities function most effectively. What conditions will enhance your skills and what conditions will tend to degrade their effectiveness?

Some people, for example, feel most effective if they can immerse themselves in all the aspects of the decision, steeping thmselves in all the details and considerations. Then they relax, ease their minds, sleep on the decision, and let the intuitive powers go to work before making the final choice. Others prefer to be quite explicit, writing everything down, discussing it with associates, and attacking the decision in a highly analytic fashion. You may want to test these and, perhaps, other methods.

It seems clear that there are some conditions which are rather dependably poor for making decisions. The pressure of deadlines, being swamped with information and alternatives, extreme emotional involvement, anxiety, regret, fear of failure, frustration, insecurity, distractions, and a variety of physical and psychological stressors. To identify one's tolerance for these things and to compensate for them where necessary is an important objective. We will see more of these adversities in Chapter 7.

Key Behaviors

It is likely that there are a few key behaviors that can most profitably be looked for in the data of your track record. If most of us could identify and cope with these few patterns, it seems probable that the payoff would be significant. In any case, let the question of complex and subtle investigations into your market behavior wait at least until you've checked on a few basics. Try looking for things like:

Not having a clear expression of what you expect from a commitment.

Doing something which is not a part of your GRS program.

Taking a flyer "just this once."

Refusing to take a loss.

Sticking with a stock which has done well in the past but ceased to perform acceptably in more recent periods.

Falling in love.

Discouragement, frustration, giving up, and various defensive reactions to "failures," losses, and poor progress.

Worrying about what others would think of what you're doing. Concern for social acceptability.

Failure to acknowledge the sort of effects the market may have on your predicting and decision making.

The important thing is to write down explicitly the kinds of hypotheses you want to test about yourself, decide what kind of data will be revealing, and decide in advance how you would interpret various outcomes.

You can, of course, plan much longer term track record experiments, testing out different investment media and different approaches to the market. You may want eventually to experiment with mutual funds, your own portfolio, trading, and so on. Once again, design the experiments carefully and keep good records. Be careful especially about undertaking radically different investment activities with great frequency. In my view you should make these kinds of experiments over periods of several years. If you're trying entirely new approaches every few months, you're probably going to learn very little of their long term effectiveness.

The System Flow Diagram

Clearly there are a great many effects, variables, hypotheses, and interactions that one might test for in his track record analysis. Start with some simple basic hypotheses that seem most interesting and useful to you. As you progress, you'll begin to get some idea of what a complex system you and the market form with your actions and interactions. Systems analysts sometimes keep rough track of complex relationships like this by means of a system flow diagram. Figure 6–1 is an example of one that I once used to see some of the things I was doing in the market. These diagrams are always far more meaningful to those who create them than to those who must untangle them, so don't worry too much about the details of mine. Basically it tries to identify some information sources and some ways of approaching the market, which in part determine the prices at which one would be willing to buy or sell various securities. Also involved is some self-awareness about one's GRS objectives and the strategy (buy and hold, dollar average) one plans to use. In addition, there is some sort of search activity which is identifying alternatives plus one's current portfolio composition and cash position. One could then compare one's action prices for buying and selling with the progress of the market and act accordingly. This diagram leaves out the ways in which the market influences my outlook

Figure 6-1

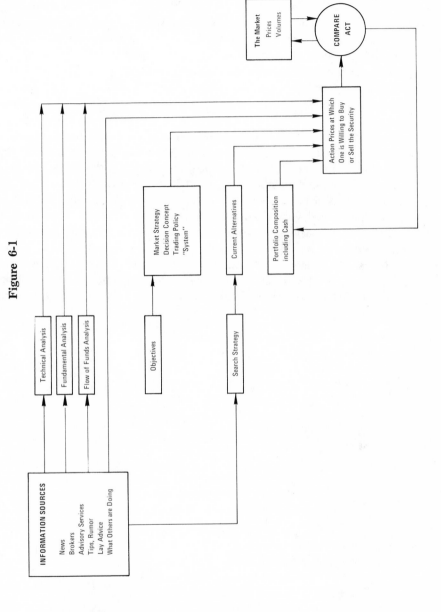

and my decision making, but these are important enough to warrant a diagram all their own. The value of these system flow diagrams is in the making of them. Try one for yourself right now, and see how difficult it is, but how revealing. Save it, and try another one after a few weeks. The comparison may give you an interesting picture of the progress of your self-awareness.

Track Record Management—A Summary

A good set of track record data is probably worth many times its weight in gold. It doesn't need to be complex. Keep it simple and keep it easy to use. Clear, organized, neatly and carefully done. Be proud of it, it's your research notebook. Keep at it. Stick with it through all the ups and downs of both the market and your emotions. It must be written or taped. It won't work if you try to remember it. What you're looking for are the dimensions of your own behavior as a financial manager and the influences which drive you. Look for a few simple behaviors, not for a lot of deep, complex, involved things. Above all, your track record must be the result of your own planning and designing. Take ideas from wherever you find them, but the conception must be yours.

7

What Makes Me Do It?

Do-it-yourself analysis. In understanding there is sal-
vation and maybe financial success. How to change
yourself by just understanding. Sticking with your
GRS plan, being comfortable with it, and facing un-
certainty fearlessly. Your experience will fool you and
you may not know it. Things you didn't really notice
in yourself but suspect in others.

Self-Analysis

Young people these days are somewhat more at ease than their
parents with the idea of the "shrink," the psychiatrist who undertakes
to help people understand what makes them do the things they do.
These young people are also probably more self-perceptive than their
parents. If they ever get interested in it, they will probably turn out
to be great at financial operations. They may find it easier than we did
to understand how there can be such a vast amount of writing about
the market, so many good investment ideas available, so many "systems"
or approaches which are not too bad, and yet there are so few people
getting rich.

Knowing, hearing, seeing, and even experiencing, are not enough to change some types of behavior. You have to take a look at yourself and appreciate what it is you are doing as you play out your part in the self-market system. But more than this, if you're going to be effectively motivated to alter your behavior, you've got to be able to explain yourself to yourself at a sufficient level of depth to give you the feeling that you understand what drives you. The key to a high probability of success in a GRS program is to objectify yourself and develop some insight into what could possibly motivate the behaviors you see. You need to become your own lay analyst and indulge yourself in the ultimate egotism of self-analysis. Nothing sophisticated, no sexual interpretations of your dreams, no talking to yourself on a couch. Just try out the hypothesis that it is often our inner needs and desires which drive us, our seeing, and our thinking. All too often, we are driven without even realizing it, and this is where the trouble starts. Wishful thinking is an old commonplace, but beyond this we need to get used to the idea that there might be wishful seeing and fearful thinking as well. Don't just get used to these ideas, but test them out as explanations of your own financial decision making.

Self-Directed Change

The idea of the efficacy of self-directed change based on self-knowledge is as contemporary as psychiatry, and yet goes back at least as far as the teaching of the Buddha. As a basic concept of psychiatry and an article of faith for Buddhists, it seems subject to very little challenge. Once a reasonable man understands some of the inner forces which shape his thought and his behavior, he is in a position to at least begin to influence what he thinks and what he does. In this sense, each of us can be the instrument of his own salvation. Our problem is not quite this grand. We want to test the more modest hypothesis that each of us has a high probability of being the instrument of his own wealth.

The more fully the origins of behavior are understood, the freer one becomes, and the more he controls his own decisions. Decision making will improve when one uses both the usual external feed back of experience and a knowledge of the internal influences on one's choosing. Decision making effectiveness is enhanced when one is freed from unconscious drives and thus finds his mental abilities operating at their highest levels. The insiduous thing about these drives is that they are, in fact, largely unconscious. They need to be brought out in the open. This understanding is the key to correction, to compensation, and thus to actually behaving in a way which will lead to the execution of a GRS program. Just knowing how is not enough.

Lots of people have great financial plans, but relatively few have whatever it is it takes to actually carry them out. Relatively few attain the poise to actually make them work. In the previous chapter we looked at some behaviors which are likely to give us trouble. We need now to see a little deeper into those patterns, to achieve a feeling that we understand them. Without this, there is a small chance that we will actually have either the will or the skill to alter our behavior. This is the basic, if highly oversimplified, notion of psychiatry. We are not going to be psychiatrists, yet enough of their ideas are in the public domain to make a little self-analysis a realistic possibility. Perhaps you will want to take the view that what first aid is to medicine, self-analysis is to psychiatry. If you have some idea what you're doing, at least the patient won't get any worse.

Sermons

In this chapter you will probably get the feeling that I am giving little sermons. I won't say don't take them personally. If you don't, they won't help much. But if it's any comfort to you, remember that I'm talking to myself as well as to you. If you had my problems . . .

We'll try to understand in some depth five types of financial behavior. A reminder first in the form of a word of caution from two famous and fascinating figures in the world of psychology, A. H. Maslow and Gordon Allport. "Just try to understand your behavior, don't try too hard to cure yourself." Remember the law of reversed effect. The harder you try to deliberately change yourself, the less effective you are likely to be. It is far more important to see and understand one's defensive responses than it is to be in a hurry to develop more constructive ones. Relax, be patient. There is a soaking effect. You may be surprised at the way understanding seems to lead to change and compensation without a lot of deliberate effort on your part.

We are sufficiently creative to generate an almost endless variety of behaviors which turn out to be inconsistent with our financial aspirations. We are very good at messing ourselves up. We will take a look behind just a few of the ways we do this, choosing those types of behavior which are something like our most frequent sources of regret as we look back at what we have done to ourselves.

Dumping the Plan

Let us suppose you had worked out what you take to be a reasonable GRS program. The probability that you will actually get rich is the probability that the plan would succeed if followed, multiplied by the probability that you will actually follow the plan. The position we have taken is that the first of these probabilities is high if your objectives correspond to what we have called getting rich slowly. We have also been arguing that the most common reason people don't get rich is their failure to actually follow a GRS plan. Pious exhortations about the virtues of sticktoitiveness seldom help. The ethic of conservative thrift, saving a little bit every pay day, may help some, but most of us will need still more help than this.

The really tough decisions are those which have to be made again and again, and seem to get no easier for the practice. We find no mode of action which can simultaneously satisfy our conflicting desires. We want to get very rich, very quickly, with a very high probability of success. We are pulled in opposite directions and the search for some sort of resolution drags on. We can discover no way of having one think we want very much, without giving up something else that we want very much. It may help to know that psychologists call this a conflict situation. At least it means that they have seen others with this kind of a problem, and we have some company throughout the human race in our misery.

We find ourselves subjected to a continuing barrage of GRQ propositions. Brokers, friends, and a vast quantity of printed words keep these before us all the time.

We find that carrying out a GRS plan is a maddeningly slow process, often a fairly dull one, and sometimes requiring more effort, patience, and self-discipline than seems reasonable to us.

For long periods our GRS results may be small or even negative. We fall behind in our planned objectives, we feel frustrated, and we sense the futility of the whole stupid idea. We alternate between wanting to give up the entire ridiculous business of getting rich, and wanting to plunge into every GRQ opportunity that comes along.

Other people tell us how very well their investments are doing, and we have no story to top theirs, perhaps no story that's even in their league. The whole market is going strongly upward, but the performance of our portfolio is totally unspectacular. Even if we're not normally envious, we begin to wonder.

We get distracted by other interests, the challenges of the job, the family, or the golf course. The notion of a GRS program occupies less and less of our attention and our energy. Eventually, it begins to seem a little silly, or unimportant, or just another of our many passing New Year's resolutions. Suddenly, something brings us up short. The oldest child is almost ready for college. It's too late to revive the old GRS plan, something has got to be done in a hurry.

Conflict

The friendly neighborhood psychologist says it's a conflict situation indeed. We are still hung up on the urge to get rick quickly and get rich surely. The GRQ experiment of Chapter 2 either didn't work very well, or its effects have worn off. We are still unable to accept the notion that if we want to do it quickly, there's a low probability of success. If we want a high probability of success, we'll have to do it slowly. We find no way out. This kind of conflict is a near relative, in its effects, of the stress-generated conditions of anxiety and frustration. Like anxiety and frustration, conflict is an internal state which is usually associated with a degradation in our decision making abilities, our poise, and our reasonableness.

The tensions which are connected with our inability to make a difficult choice and then live comfortably with it, produce a variety of adjustive reactions and activate an array of defense mechanisms. We respond, largely without realizing it, to that inner urge to relieve the pressure.

Look through the following small catalog of reactions to conflict and see if you experience any flashes of insight into yourself. See if there is any clue among these adjustments and defenses, to understanding your doings at a deeper level.

Fantasy, unreality — At last I've found a GRQ proposition which is different, this really is a "sure thing"; there are other ways that I can get rich beside slowly; one of these days it will just happen to me.

Repression — Money isn't everything, perhaps it isn't anything; we'll buy a little chicken farm and grow all our own food; suppress the probabilities, ignore the risks; have the courage to take a real flyer, tomorrow we'll either have it made or . . .

Fixated search — Keep on looking, work even harder at finding the sure thing GRQ proposition; all the experience we've had and all the failures really don't prove a thing, just a litle bad luck, keep after it; it's there at the end of the rainbow.

Goal substitution — Let's take much higher risks, accept much lower probabilities of success; this country wasn't built by people who were afraid to take risks; "no guts, no glory"; let's lower our whole notion of "rich," we really don't need to maintain our standard of living at this ridiculous present level; if you can't make it really big, forget it; give the whole thing up and live for today.

Reorganizing one's view to set the conflict in a new and less significant perspective — All this money-grubbing is cutting into my golf game; let's enjoy today, tomorrow we will cope with tomorrow, which, after all, may never come; we have no business making these financial decisions anyway, let's turn it over to a hired professional; we're too young to be worrying that far ahead.

Post hoc resolution of cognitive dissonance — We really didn't want to get rich anyway; we're happy just the way we are; the whole thing is foolish and we knew that before we ever got involved; the smart way to make money is to put more effort into the job, not messing around in the stock market; my father lost his shirt in 1929 and the only smart thing to do is buy government bonds.

There is, in addition to conflict, a kind of shock effect which occurs when we go from just making a GRS plan to actually implementing it. We discover, that carrying it out involves a far greater emotional involvement than we had expected. There is risk to which we are not accustomed, pressure from the family to divert funds to other purposes, and often a surprising degree of personal involvement. We find ourselves anxious, fearful of failure, awakening new needs for achievement, and seeing difficulties as personal threats.

All of these combine to make us less capable of clear and complex thought, less poised and sure of our decisions, less able to respond reasonably to information and to the results of our efforts. When you feel about to dump the plan, take a look at yourself with the aid of some of these hypotheses. If you can understand what you're doing, you'll be in charge of yourself again.

Going To Bed With It
(And Sleeping With It)

Most stock market advice begins with the proposition that before you put a penny into the market, you ought to take care of all your rainy day and insurance needs. Nobody ever knows, however, how much insurance is enough or how many rainy days one ought reasonably to be prepared for. Money that you use in the stock market ought to be, it is prudently suggested, money that you can afford to risk or money that you can afford to lose. The first of these phrases will appear so imprecise as to be useless, if you've begun to think about risk and be explicit about it. The second, has a kind of nonsensical ring to it. Money is far too serious a matter for most of us to feel that we can afford to lose any of it. We worked too hard to get it to respond sensibly to that advice.

Generally speaking, if one has formulated a GRS plan and achieved a comfortable level of insurance protection against the leading risks that are of concern, all of one's remaining funds should be committed to the plan. The key is to insure to a comfortable degree against risks which actively concern you. The function of insurance, the really important function, is to put your mind at ease so that you can use it for other purposes. Insure to the extent that you free yourself from worry, and then put the rest of your funds into your GRS program. This doesn't mean, of course, that all of your funds should be invested all the time. Some may very well be in cash, and this portion may vary greatly according to one's plans and the progress of the market. Funds committed to the plan determine the overall scale of your objectives, your planning horizon, and the level of risk required. The important phrase is "committed to the plan." Here is where the "money you can afford to lose" people really have a point.

If you have all of your remaining funds in a program you can't sleep with, you're in a bad spot. Unless you're relaxed, comfortable, confident, interested, and well informed about your commitments, you begin to lose the cool, detached rationality of the professional. If you develop a high level of anxiety about your funds, if you are losing sleep over your portfolio, if you're calling several times a day for the latest price quotations, the pressure is building up. This is the sort of psychological pressure which will make you a very poor judge of how to manage your GRS program. Anxiety is well known to be a degrading influence on our decision making abilities. If what the market did during the day determines your mood in the evening, and the amount of sleep you get, you'll probably ruin your life at home and your effectiveness on the job. It will almost surely mean that something will very soon cause you to depart from your GRS program.

Anxiety

Anxiety is a psychological tension which results from a fear of failure or a need to avoid the personal consequences of defeat. Our reaction to the stress of self-imposed demands for results, or achievements, may take the form of a sort of generalized apprehension toward the future. We develop a great personal stake in the outcome of every financial commitment, and the possibility of failure becomes the possibility of a serious loss of our sense of self-worth. This free-floating, unattached, vague, non-directed feeling is not a fear of something definite. It is rather a tendency to view each financial operation as a test of personal worth and a proving ground for one's worthiness of self-respect once more. Anxiety, as is rather well established, operates to interfere with thinking, with concentration, and with reasonable and coherent choices. If you have a capacity for worry and are consistently anxious, you have an excellent opportunity to enhance your financial effectiveness.

We should be very careful not to take on the mantle of the lay analyst, nor to pretend to offer explanations in depth of the sources and mechanisms of anxiety. Yet its presence is not overly subtle and the possibility of mitigating its milder forms seems readily at hand. We are not talking about neurotic or psychotic anxiety, but rather about its lesser and more common forms. We find ourselves habitually worried, apprehensive, and yet unable to say clearly the source or object of this feeling.

In the Face of Adversity

Anxiety is one of a number of psychological adversities which lead to unproductive, irrational defense mechanisms. To simply appreciate this possibility is to take the first step toward more reasoned responses to it. What can one learn about his own tolerance for stress and the nature of his defensive reactions?

Slight anxiety may heighten our abilities and enhance our performance, but severe anxiety produces quite different results. We may find ourselves postponing or avoiding decisions, becoming rigid in the way we choose, and very prone to the suppression of uncertainty. We may notice ourselves favoring safe, failure-free opportunities, even though they may not be consistent with our objectives. Unconsciously we repress those feelings and experiences which arouse our anxiety. There is a lack of spontaneity in our conceptualizing, and a serious reduction in our ability to create and improvise.

The most important consequence of anxiety, however, is that it is the very sort of psychological adversity which most seriously impairs the functioning of our intuition. It is one of the results of stress which leaves the natural and unaided processes of the individual most degraded and least effective. We become unadaptive and stereotyped in our responses; irritable, distracted, and generally ineffective as learners and thinkers. The best professionals are probably well aware of their tendencies toward anxiety and their abilities to tolerate it.

To approach professionalism and to have a high probability of actually carrying through your plan, you must not only put some real effort into designing it yourself, you must like it enough to be able to sleep with it.

Comfort and Commitment

If you have a GRQ proposition with a low probability of big, quick gains, you have to live with the high probability of quick losses. If you have all of your funds committed, these may be big quick losses and you'll have to try to get through each night with the thought that all of your family's financial progress and security are involved. This is almost certain to keep you awake, raise your anxiety level to intolerable heights, and make you a seriously irrational financial manager. You're at exactly the opposite emotional pole from the unpressured professional who is managing somebody else's money with detachment and objectivity. He should be managing yours as well.

The more comfortable you are with your GRS program, the more of your funds you should commit to it. If you're still testing the GRS hypothesis, keep your commitments small. If your GRS program is moving along, if you're feeling pretty much unpressured by it, increase your stake in it. As it grows, you should also reduce the amount of commercial insurance you carry, putting the premiums thus saved into your GRS program. It makes a lot of sense to insure yourself to a gradually increasing degree, as your capital grows. Most people begin to do this by dropping the very expensive collision insurance on their cars. The criterion of how fast to move toward self-insurance is strictly in terms of your anxieties and your mental comfort. Remember the most important function of insurance is to keep your mind operating at its highest level of effectiveness, which means as free from anxieties as is reasonably possible. Don't do anything you can't sleep with.

Worry, anxiety, and fear are not just going to make you tired, miserable, and ulcerated. They are going to destroy your professional poise as a decision maker and greatly reduce your chances of sticking with your GRS program. This is the really important reason why your plans and your commitments have to match your personality, your self-image, and your tolerance for psychological pressures. The ideal is to develop a GRS program which isn't on your mind too much of the time, which you can attend to effectively with short periods of deliberate concentration, and which doesn't keep intruding on your much-needed periods of mental relaxation.

Leaping Without Enough Looking

In our financial operations we seldom leap without any looking. The problem is usually a little more subtle. We sometimes look too little before we leap and sometimes we look too much. The symptoms show up in our track record analysis when we begin to compare our results with our decisions.

We see ways that we could clearly have avoided some of our unsatisfactory results, if only we had spent a little more effort on the decision process.

We notice some good opportunities that we passed up, and it begins to appear that with some additional attention we might have avoided this.

We are getting good results that seem, in all honesty, to be just plain lucky.

There is in many of us a deep need for certainty. A need to know what will happen if we make a commitment, and a need to avoid situations which involve the unknown, are basic to our nature. We have a strong habit, a tradition, and a social custom, of not being explicit about uncertainty. We see single futures, not only because this simplifies our decisions, but because it tends to serve our inner needs.

Need effects play subtle and unnoticed roles in our ways of predicting. The need for certainty causes us to see it, to suppress uncertainty, to search too long, to gather too much data, and to hope in vain for something that will bring a dramatic reduction in our uncertainty. Hoping and wishing lead us toward assuming the future will be as we wish it rather than toward the expression of our real uncertainty. The desire for clairvoyance may lead us to pretend it.

We have a need to preserve the comfortable habit of dealing with predictions in which the uncertainty has been suppressed. We tend to confirm the assurances we would like to have about the future by overlooking all the little things that might go wrong and stand between us and our expectations. We need to preserve the self-image of strength, positive conviction, and self-assurance which we associate with the top manager, the gunslinger, the big financial operator. Needs drive us to assume that we know the future and if one knows the future, there is little point in gathering more information about it.

Taking a Loss

We buy something, often with quite a clear prediction of when and by about how much it will go up. It goes down and stays there. At first we think this is simply some slight unforeseen aberration and that our expectations will turn out to be correct after all. Slowly, predicting turns to hoping. Then hoping for the originally anticipated gain turns to hoping the stock will simply return to where we bought it so that we may get out even. The need to get even takes hold and we wait, meanwhile other opportunities come and go. If the wait goes on long enough, the pressures of frustration begin to have their effect. We become discouraged, filled with self-doubts, and perhaps decide that if we can only get out even, we'll never buy stock again. It's a classic behavior pattern, showing up with great regularity among inexperienced financial managers. Why?

Two interesting concepts serve often to muddy the waters by emphasizing the divergence between the logical you and the psychological you. The notion that somehow paper losses and paper profits are different from realized losses and realized profits bothers many of us. Let us set aside tax considerations as we have regularly done, since in the eyes of IRS it's only realized profits or losses that mean anything. Suppose you're holding something which has gone down. Are you tempted to comfort yourself and preserve your self-esteem by taking the view that a loss is not a loss until you sell? It's only a paper loss. If you're not actually contemplating the decision of whether or not to sell the stock, if no *action* is being considered, then what you think of the position of the stock has no decision making consequences. If, however, you're actually entertaining the question of whether or not to sell, then the original price has absolutely no relevance for decision making purposes. The choice is whether to hold, or whether to sell at the current price and put the proceeds to other uses. The criterion is to choose so as to maximize the probability of achieving your desired level of performance. Will the probability be greater if we hold the present stock or if we liquidate our position and do something else with the funds? What we originally paid for the stock has no relevance, it plays no part in your decisions and their future consequences. What you paid for the stock is called a sunk cost. There's absolutely nothing you can do about it now. It's in the past. Your decision is about what to do in the present and the future consequences of your actions. Sunk costs don't enter into the decision process at all, logically. Psychologically, all sorts of people have trouble accepting the sunk cost principle, including a great many responsible and experienced managers. It's very hard to divorce one's self from what was paid for a stock months, or even years ago.

Needs again help us to understand what we are doing. We are driven by the need for self-justification, to preserve our self-esteem, to avoid admitting a personal mistake, and the need to avoid threats to our self-respect. Somehow as long as we don't actually take the loss, as long as we can defuse it by calling it a paper loss, we can justify ourselves and our expectations. While logically we can see that what's done is done, and the thing to do now is look ahead, psychologically, this involves such a personal challenge that it is close to impossible for us to achieve.

Until we actually take the loss, it may be possible to avoid admitting to ourselves and to others, that things have not turned out the way we had expected. We may change our anticipations for the stock in a classic example of adjusting our beliefs to reduce the dissonance between what we think and what is actually happening. If something goes down during a period when we expected it to go up, we take a new view of its prospects, concluding perhaps that it will surely go up, but over a somewhat longer time horizon than we had at first supposed. To make a new prediction of this sort, puts us at ease with the situation in which we find ourselves.

We may not be willing to take a loss until we have some way of rationalizing what has happened, some way of shifting the blame from ourselves to unfriendly circumstances or unwise advisors. We may postpone a loss because if we take it we are confronted by the next problem, what to do with the funds thus released. This is a problem which may seem most easily solved by holding on.

Frustration

The psychological stress of a losing position, a defeat, a demonstration of personal shortcoming, tends to degrade our effectiveness as decision makers. The frustration we experience provokes us into aggression against ourselves and others. One way to handle this is to drastically reduce our goals, resulting in the very common reaction to hold on until we get even and then get out of the market for good. The psychological stress of frustration prevents us from reasonably attending to what might be the more productive alternatives than simply holding our position. Frustration is intensified by our failure to see that a loss is fully consistent with reasonable prior anticipations. Had we been fully explicit about our prediction for the stock, we would have noted in our track record that there was indeed some probability of a loss. Its occurrence would then seem less surprising, less contradictory of our judgment, and would be far more likely to produce a constructive reaction. To be explicit about the probability of a loss tends to depersonalize the event if it occurs, to avoid the onset of severe self-doubts, and to prevent the seeming destruction of one's financial plans. To be clear about the probability of a loss is to prepare for it, to visualize one's possible reactions to it, and to develop in advance, plans for useful responses to it.

The higher one's goals, the greater one's need for achievement, the greater, as a consequence, will be the emotional impact of a losing position. The nearer one's planning horizon, the greater the time pressure one feels to achieve successful performance, and thus the stronger one's reaction to a losing position. One of the essential marks of progress in the development of your GRS program is an emerging understanding of your tolerance for stress and an ability to predict your reactions to it.

Experience is the Great Teacher,
But Not Always

Experience is much honored as the great teacher, but, like most teachers, it has those pupils of which it is not particularly proud. There are those who persistently attempt to get rich quick and persistently fail, those who can never escape the spell of hunches, tips, rumors, or transcendental meditation, and those who give it all up after one unsatisfying venture. In financial matters, as perhaps no other area of personal decision making, the simple, beautiful notion that we learn best from experience needs to get the hard-nosed treatment. Most people have no track record at all and their recollection of their experience is vague, highly selective, and almost totally unanalyzed for useful implications. To have a written track record, set down with some attempt at objectivity, and examined with a dispassionate curiosity about one's self, is to have taken a major step toward utilizing experience. Experience should be used carefully since it is likely to be expensive. Much of what I have been saying aims at exposing the static which interferes with the signals experience has for us.

Our needs, the drives for self-esteem, for self-justification, for achievement, and for success, are very much in our way when we try to read the messages of our experience. The worst part of the problem is that we are seldom aware of what they are doing to us. Experience is not such a great teacher in our personal financial operations unless we can begin to notice the ways in which we interpret and distort it to make it easier to take. Experience is not all beautiful and we have subtle, unsuspected ways of making it more appealing to ourselves. Each of the behaviors we have tried to look into can best be seen as a way in which our responses to experience, our emotional defenses make it difficult for us to learn from it. Quite without realizing it, we distort the world to help reduce our own tensions. What we cannot fix externally, we tend to fix internally by seeing things as we would like them to be.

When we undertake to learn from our financial operations, we almost always focus on what is "out there." We look at the market, the economy, the external world, and almost never at our internal world. Experience seems like something which happens to us, not something in which we participate as an interacting component. This makes it especially difficult to step aside and see ourselves rationalizing our losses, protecting

ourselves by transfering blame, taking comfort from the fact that everybody is in the same boat, and telling ourselves that nobody could have
foreseen what has happened to our commitments.

The more general question of the conditions under which one can
learn most effectively from experience has not been widely studied.
Those who seem to have had the oldest interest in this problem are
the sages who developed Eastern religions such as Buddhism and
Taoism. These men gave considerable thought to "freeing the mind"
or creating the conditions under which one's intuition could work most
effectively. The familiar progression in Yoga from concentration to meditation and contemplation is aimed at freeing the mind from irrational
passions, unconscious needs, and all manner of distractions so that it
may be most reasonable. It is particularly fascinating that many of the
findings of contemporary psychology tend to confirm the notions developed by these ancient thinkers. It seems to me that both would agree
on the point that what is needed is self-knowledge or self-awareness
in our financial operations.

Wishful thinking is our common phrase for the sort of distortion
that creeps into our perceiving and conceptualizing as a result of basic
needs and desires. We ought to work at taking a tough-minded view
of this need-determined sort of distortion because we ourselves are
usually not conscious of it, and may even deny its existence with some
vigor.

Habits

Habitual ways of viewing a situation arise because a conception
which meets the needs of one situation is uncritically applied to others.
Habits might be thought of as ways of economizing the limited capacity
of the mind. Rather than develop a conception which tries to account
objectively for each individual financial situation, one simply resorts by
analogy to customary conceptions or tends to fit decisions into categories
previously developed. Organizations develop such habits and they tend
to get formalized into policies or routines for decision making. These
habitual conceptions are perpetuated because they satisfy one's need
to respond to the pressure of affairs which overtax the conceptualizing
capacity of the mind. Habits also help to satisfy the need for being able
to defend a decision. A widely used rationalization for an unsuccessful
decision is the claim that it was based on "the way I always do it."

Satisfying Thoughts

One's conceptions tend to move toward a view of the situation as
the person would like to see it, and not necessarily as it is. Expectations

are not independent of desires and conceptions play a part in satisfying needs when actions prove inadequate to the task. If we find ourselves in very limited control of a situation, to some extent quite powerless to act in a satisfying way, then at least we can remake our conceptualization of the situation so as to view it more satisfactorily. If our need for certainty and confidence cannot be achieved through predictive knowledge and the ability to control events, then perhaps our conceptions will become subjectively free of doubt and uncertainty in response to this need.

Perception is a selective process which tends to give structure to the vastly complicated situations encountered in our experience. In perceiving a situation, some elements of it "stand out" more clearly than others. The term is "figure and ground," the figure being those elements perceived most clearly against the suppressed background of the remainder. The elements which tend to stand out as figure are at least in part controlled by needs, in the sense of having previously been perceived in satisfying situations. This, of course, works as the result of fears as well as desires.

Social Sharing

Finally, conceptions get distorted because of the social processes which lead us to view things in ways accepted by our associates. Socially shared views, which come not so much from contact with reality as from the need to agree, to belong, or to avoid questioning the views of a group, are part of most interpretations of our experience.

An individual in a society experiences a demand from his fellows that his behavior be reliable, predictable, and in a general sense within control. He needs the acceptance that comes with conforming. They need to know how he is going to make decisions so they can account for, and plan on, the basis of his behavior. He thus finds it increasingly necessary to conform to the society's way of conceptualizing decision situations or to follow the conventional rules. The rules and conventions tend to become important, no longer because of their original objective effectiveness for achieving goals but rather for their own sake as social criteria. This leads to viewing financial opportunities as falling into one or another of a relatively small number of socially sanctioned categories. Thus, our conceptualization of choice situations becomes a rigid process. This may mean the decisions are less and less successful at the same time they are becoming more reliable, predictable, and socially defensible.

Few of us are free from the need for social acceptance, for approval, and for the achievement and preservation of social status. We would prefer to avoid criticism and receive full credit for our accomplishments.

Does this need cause us to see things the way they are seen by our friends and those whom we respect? Do we see as desirable actions which are likely to be acceptable to those whose approval we would like to have? Clearly we may do this consciously and deliberately, but the more troublesome instances are those in which it occurs without our really suspecting it. The socially shared distortions of perception, the errors we pursue because everybody seems to see things that way, are troublesome only when we are not sufficiently self-aware to see what is happening. Do we see as best a course of action which, likely to reflect credit on us no matter what happens, or one which permits us, seemingly in all reason and good conscience, to shift the blame for failure to others? Do we tend to reflect on our past decisions in ways which are self-justifying, explaining away our failures and congratulating ourselves on the skillful brilliance of our successes? Do we find ourselves, for example, interested in a stock simply because those whom we admire claim to be buying it? There are many such ways in which, quite beyond our realization, our social relationships exert influences which creep into our perceptions. The classic example is the subject in the experiment who is asked to look at a small light in a dark room. After a time, another person in the room remarks confidently that the light is moving. The subject soon reports that he too sees the light moving, although in fact it is stationary.

Emotional Distortions

Beyond the realm of our inner needs, there are other ways in which our perceptions mislead us if they are left unexamined and unsuspected. We tend, for example, to see other people and situations in terms of the emotions we are currently experiencing and the traits which we ourselves possess. We may see our feelings and desires as being shared by others. We see others as interested when we are interested, and as frustrated when we ourselves are frustrated. We become especially sensitive to undesirable personality traits in others when we ourselves possess them. We magnify the failures of others when they fail in ways which we have experienced. Most of us are more than sufficiently self-aware to see our general moods of optimism and pessimism reflected in the way we perceive financial situations.

There is the long known "halo effect" which is a good example of a way of simplifying our complex experience. We sometimes use a general impression of a company as a halo which prevents us from seeing its specific traits very clearly. We may single out one feature and use it as a basis for judging others. We see a firm whose product we like as also having a good management and achieving high earnings. We tend to see a firm which does well in one business as doing well in another. If some aspect of a financial situation is favorable, it may color our evaluation of other aspects of the situation. We may link quite unrelated factors in forming judgments, as we do when we find ourselves favoring a particular stock because we admire the style of the issuing firm's office building.

Our perceptions are likely to fall under the influences of the order in which data comes to us. Our first impressions of people and financial opportunities do tend to last. Many of us have noticed that the first person who takes a strong position in discussing a highly ambiguous financial situation, very often takes us right along with him in his particular categorizing of the situation. There is, however, not only this priority effect, but sometimes a recency effect as well. We tend sometimes to give more weight to the last things we have seen, the last viewpoint that had been expressed, and the last experience we have had.

A good deal of our perception of the market situations we face is likely to be through the eyes of others. Most of us become pretty good at compensating for the selective perceptions of familiar friends who frequently bring us information. Most of us also sense when we are being "conned" or "sold." In these situations, we can adjust our responses with some effectiveness. The problems arise when we, without seeing what we are doing, respond to the color and binding of a report, the accent of an informant, or the skill with which an associate can manipulate the language.

Why We Do It—A Summary

The influence of our needs on our perception and thinking constitute one of the most serious sources of difficulty in our learning from experience. Our needs for wish-fulfillment, escape, or self-defense may be sources of difficulty largely because we are not aware of their distorting effects on our decision making. Vigilance, self-knowledge, self-awareness or self-conciousness constitute the basic strategy for freeing ourselves from the subconscious sources of distortion. Knowing oneself makes it easier to see financial situations accurately, but knowing oneself in this sense is not easy.

There is considerable evidence indicating that our cognitive abilities are significantly impaired and degraded by stress. Our thinking or conceptualizing skills appear to suffer, perhaps quite seriously, under both physiological stress, such as fatigue, and under psychological stress. The kinds of psychological stress which may influence our decision making include: high personal risk, pressures for success, emotional involvement, fear of failure, need to achieve, anxiety, and time pressures. Strong internal drives have the effect on some of us of reducing our ability to relate and structure the information available in our track records.

Concentration, or at least freedom from distraction, is the essential precondition for most complex decision making. Our emotional responses to stress such as, anger, dislike, annoyance, or frustration often act quite without our being aware of them. They influence our conceptualizing in ways which we may later have cause to regret. We admire the cool, detached, unemotional financial manager who has a high tolerance for stress.

We need to be prepared for some rather subtle effects which may come from exposure to these ideas. None of us is likely to memorize them, indeed, most of us are likely to forget them in a rather short time. Somewhat surprisingly, however, the effects are likely to be there as we go about the business of making financial decisions. There is interesting evidence that one is more likely to "discover" things about himself and about his decisions if he has had a look at these kinds of hypotheses. They give us a kind of readiness to learn from experience that is not at a conscious level, but somehow permits us to learn more quickly and more effectively. Even though we may not have these ideas on the tips of our tongues, they make it more likely that we will be able to think effectively about decisions, rather than have to rely on trial and error. This increased sensitivity seems to make us more likely to actually *formulate* hypotheses about our interaction with the market and by this means to move more rapidly toward greater understanding of our behavior. Thus there is likely to be a certain payoff from looking at these ideas, almost in spite of ourselves.

If you are able to begin interpreting yourself to yourself in these terms, you may well find that your financial operations take on the coolness, detachment, objectivity, and reasonableness which form the real advantages of the professional financial manager. The unemotional quality of your planning gives it a professional air which is likely to bring an interesting increase in your chances of actually carrying through your GRS program.

8

Need, Greed, and Goal Dynamics

The trouble with just running up the score. Setting goals in terms of consumption rather than balance sheet figures. Trading-off is tough. How to succeed and fail successfully. The grand old sayings that may do you wrong.

The Money Trap

If you think of your objective as one of simply accumulating a great deal of money you may be in trouble already. The probability of success for your GRQ program may not be very high. To set as a goal the amassing of a large liquid fortune is to face a good chance of becoming involved in the "liquidity dilemma." Money, without question, has the great advantage of liquidity, it can be turned into most anything. As some people see it, it can be turned into absolutely anything. Yet if we think and plan exclusively in terms of money as we formulate goals and study our drives, we fall into a kind of trap. We begin to simply keep score with money, and once this begins, it is very likely that we will become involved in piling up the score as an end in itself. We want more and more money, not for what we can do with it, but for the sake of having more money. Modern psychology has confirmed the ancient wisdom that some wants are satiable but some are not. It is all too easy for many of us to fall into the difficulty of finding that our need for money is not one of those that can be satisfied. Even worse, "the more you get, the more you want" is an effect which is a disastrous possibility for some of us: A GRS program with no stable finite goal has almost no chance of success at all. It leads one into ever more risky situations in the effort to seek even higher returns, and thus we face increasing probabilities of failure. The love of money may not be the root of *all* evil, but it is a real detriment to the chances of success for our GRS program.

Once again, here are some hypotheses that must be tested by each of you individually. The concept of emergent needs goes something like this. There is a hierarchy of needs which operate in a precedence relationship. When our physical needs for food and shelter have been satisfied, other needs emerge which occupy our attention and motivate our behavior. Until we have taken care of food and shelter, however, these physical needs take precedence over all others. The next set of needs to emerge may be the social needs which have to do with our acceptance by others and our dependence on them. After we achieve some degree of satisfaction of the social needs, our ego needs emerge. We turn our attention to our achievements and our needs for personal fulfillment. Some of us behave as if money was not simply a potential satisfier of these needs, but a need in itself. Having achieved one level of wealth, a new need for more wealth merges, and on and on. The need for money occupies our attention rather completely, and begins to dominate our behavior. There is little opportunity for other needs to emerge.

The old notion of "the more you get, the more you want," seems to be quite consistent with many modern studies of behavior, and is important for anticipating the ways in which our own behavior can upset a GRS program. If we can predict our reactions, perhaps we can control them or compensate for them to some degree. We can imagine two rough stereotypes for need-emergence patterns. Money makes some people more conservative, less willing to take risks, more interested in holding on tightly to what they have accumulated. As their wealth grows, they become more and more concerned about probabilities of loss. They tend to shift their financial operations toward opportunities which have lower expected performance, but also lower probability of loss in their view. Perhaps these people have something rather definite in mind that they want to do with their money. They are operating so as to maximize the probability of achieving that fund which is sufficient to do what they want to do.

The other stereotype is, of course, the person who having made $1000 will try for $100,000, and if he makes $100,000 will try for $1,000,-000. He may have very little idea what he wants to do with this money other than just have it. He may not give much thought to how it could be translated into satisfying forms other than simply figures on his adding machine tape. Here the pattern becomes one of risking larger and larger amounts of money and accepting lower and lower probabilities of success, in the hope of higher and higher rates of return. This is clearly the road back to the increasing probabilities of disaster which we associated with attempts to get rich quick. Nothing could be more useful than to sense the possibility of this type of behavior in ourselves, and by sensing it, have the poise, the self-perception to avoid it.

If your objective is "to make a lot of money" you are probably in trouble from the beginning. You are far better off to set a series of goals which are definite and related to ways in which you hope to use the money. In this way, you avoid the tendency and the temptation to expose yourself to risks which are not warranted by the value of the possible gains. You avoid becoming involved in opportunities which have a high probability of leaving you with nothing.

How to Set Your Goals

First, go back to Chapter 1 and look again at the trade-off problem. Recall that the amount of money you are shooting for, the time horizon, and the probability of success are interrelated in the least desirable of all possible ways. The more money you're after, the lower the probability of success. The more money you want to amass, the longer it is likely to take. The sooner you want to achieve your goal, the lower your chances of success. Things couldn't be worse. Try the experiment on pages 129–131.

It's easy enough to know what is good, but very difficult when you have to begin giving up one good thing to achieve another. The tough part of the problem is the trading off of time, financial objective, and chances of success. Somewhat unfortunately, it's a completely personal problem. Others can only point out the problem and help you to see its structure. It may be very helpful to learn how things are interrelated. Recall from Chapter 1 our discussion of the compounding effect which indicates the highly non-linear relationship between time and financial objectives. Recall also, the general view that if you want higher expected performance, you will find yourself accepting higher risks, or higher chances of not achieving your objective. It may be helpful to be quite explicit about a basic policy for making decisions consistent with one's value system. For a given financial objective, at a given future point in time, we should seek to maximize the probability of success. This kind of policy doesn't solve the trade-off problem, but it helps prevent one from falling into inconsistent commitments from time to time.

Facing It

The trade-off problem is sufficiently difficult that there is a tendency to ignore it, suppress it, or give it up as impossible. Clearly, when we make financial decisions and work out GRS programs, we are acting as if we had some implied trade-off relationships. The effort that may be required to gradually make these more and more explicit as one progresses in self-awareness is an effort which many have found rewarding. It is the kind of effort now being undertaken with some considerable success in business and government by systems analysts. Another sort of attempt to side step the trade-off problem is to keep on searching for an opportunity which is so good in all respects that one really doesn't have to give up anything in order to get something else. That is, to keep hoping that we will discover an opportunity that will result in a lot of money, very quickly, with a high probability of success. This, of course, is nothing more than our old friend the GRQ opportunity. Face the trade-off problem directly, but be patient with yourself. With time and attention, you will come to know what you want with increasing clarity.

Your Priorities

Next, stop thinking, for a while at least, in terms of money. Think instead of what you want to achieve with your money and when you want to do it. Do a little mental simulation of your future. Be explicit about the things that you hope money will do for you and for your family. Are you concerned about medical emergencies, about education, travel, retirement, taking care of your parents, or changing your life style? Put some priorities on these things. Make up a rank ordered list. This in itself may be a very difficult job, but it is the best possible first step. Now complicate your rank ordering by asking yourself how you would space these things out in time if you can't achieve them all at once. You want some protection against medical emergencies almost immediately, you'd like to travel before you're old enough to retire, but only after you've gotten the children through college, and so on. Try to make some rough predictions of what you will most want five years or ten years from now. What kinds of desires will grow and what kinds will fade? You won't, after you've struggled with these questions, end up with anything like a nice neat solution to the trade-off problem. You will, however, most likely have made some very interesting progress toward finding out what it is you want in the way that is useful for planning and decision making. Until one takes a cut at the trade-off problem, one can't be said to know what one wants in any very useful sense.

If, for example, you're interested in retirement, pick two or three retirement dates, differing by several years. Then pick two or three retirement life styles; perhaps your present life style, one involving lots of travel, and one involving a quiet existence in some small community in the sun. Make some rough calculations of the amounts of money that would be required to support each of these life styles. Translate this into the annual performance that would be necessary to take your present capital and your subsequent additions to capital, up to the various required amounts at each of the three retirement dates you are considering. Finally, think hard about the probability of success for you and the market working together to achieve each of these levels of investment performance. If you do all this, the chances are you'll know a lot more about your wants than you know right now. You'll also begin to get away from the tendency to plan only in terms of dollars and thus cultivate an insatiable want.

Milestones

A final and operationally important step is to translate your goals into milestones, or intermediate goals. If you're aiming at a planning horizon which is ten years in the future and hope to reach your financial objective by achieving an annual performance of 12 percent, set down explicitly where you will have to be one year hence, two years hence, and so on. Annual milestones for review of your progress are extremely useful, say in March when you're working on your income tax or at Christmas when you get your bonus. Set up in advance some sort of plan for responding to your progress at each milestone. What to do if you're way ahead or way behind where you should be? Perhaps you should move toward less risky opportunities, or perhaps you will decide to increase the level of risk at which you will operate. There is, however, one fundamental rule about which I am quite certain. Don't change these things by chance or whim. Plan in advance the conditions under which you will want to change your plans. All of this requires a great deal more looking into the future than most of us would do, either casually or comfortably. The effort required, however, has an interesting potential for stabilizing our behavior and thus increasing the chances of success in a GRS program.

Reactions to Failure

What are you to do at a milestone review if you are pretty close to your goal for that point in time? Probably relax. Things are going fine. What do you do if you find yourself doing far better or far worse than your plans require at that point? Be very, very careful.

Suppose you come up to your first milestone and find that you are not doing very well, perhaps even losing money. There are a number of responses you might see in yourself, some of which are likely to be helpful, constructive, and functional, and some of which are likely to be somewhat the opposite, disfunctional. You feel frustrated, discouraged, defeated, personally a failure, embarrassed, angry, aggressive, and you look for some person or place on which to put the blame. You become aggressive both against yourself and against the world.

Disfunctional Reactions—Don'ts

Don't:

Decide that getting rich is not important.

Make dramatic reductions in your objectives.

Give it all up in a fit of discouragement.

Accept lower chances of success by seeking dramatically higher returns.

Blame it blindly and unanalytically on your broker, your advisory service, your approach to the market.

Take it out on your family.

Hate yourself, let your self-confidence sag.

Spend long, morose hours going over it in your mind.

Take refuge in fantasies of what might have happened if. . . .

Functional Reactions to Failure

Do:

Have some advance plan which may involve deliberately doing nothing, taking modestly greater risks, lowering your objectives slightly but not radically, or committing more of your cash reserves.

Recall that when you started, you explicitly set down the chances of success and failure, that failure at this point was something you had foreseen, that you had considered its chances of happening, and that it had been a part of your deliberate planning.

Try to work through your track record data, testing some hypotheses about yourself, the market, and your interaction with the market that may have constructive implications.

Look for things you might have foreseen but missed, things you might reasonably have done, not things that would have required a clairvoyant.

Try to put the situation in perspective, noting that even the professionals can't win them all, that this is not any sort of a demonstration of lack of personal worth on your part, and that you are picking up some of the "invaluable discipline of defeat."

How To Live With Success— Will It Spoil You?

Perhaps you arrive at a milestone to find that the net worth of your program is interestingly ahead of where you had planned to be at that point. Again some reactions you will observe in yourself are likely to be functional and some are not.

The Disfunctional Responses

Don't:

Get gluttonous, dramatically increase your goals, take significantly higher risks.

Start using your capital for cars, vacations, and other things that were not a part of your original plan of financial operations.

Make a sudden change in your life style (take a little better care of yourself, live a little for a little while, but don't get in the habit).

Assume that a recent rise in the market will go on and on, signifying a whole new era in our history.

Let yourself believe you're some kind of a wizard; some of what's happened you can take credit for, but not all of it.

Tell yourself that you can surely and consistently outrun your milestone goals in the future.

If You Succeed

Do:

Make some modest adjustments in your objectives, but nothing big (What has really changed about your wants?).

Reduce the risk slightly, moving toward higher probabilities of achieving slightly lower annual performance.

Add a little to your cash reserve.

Take a hard look at where the market is, and ask yourself if it isn't about time for it to go the other way.

Learn what you can about what you did "right" by working with your track record data.

Deflating the Platitudes, the Comfortable Sayings

It may or may not be remarkable to notice the extent to which our financial operations are dominated by platitudes, wise sayings, "common" sense, and what has come to be known as the conventional wisdom. Many of us are strongly influenced by these socially shared notions which seem like obvious lighthouses in the fog of uncertainty and ambiguity that we must confront. They not only provide an appealing and defensible way of responding to uncertainty, but they help relieve us from the cognitive strain of having to work out our own plans and goals. The tougher the decision problem, the more appealing the platitude. Some of these grand old chestnuts may be just fine for you, may turn out to be very helpful, and may seem quite sensible even after a close examination. Some of them may be the rankest baloney. A few of them I have attempted to deflate in earlier chapters, so you will know my opinion, for whatever that may be worth to you. Don't trust them very much until you have given them a sufficiently hard-nosed look to know what *you* think. Watch out for situations in which your behavior is being controlled by these platitudes without your really being conscious of it. Here are some examples to which you'll be able to add your own favorites:

Money can't buy happiness. The best things in life are free.

Don't invest until all of your other financial requirements have been met.

Only invest money that you can really afford to lose.

Aunt Martha will leave us plenty. Don't let's worry about the financial future.

When the time comes, we'll find some way to finance the kids' college education.

One of these days, we're going to take a year off and take a trip around the world.

By the time I retire, I expect to have a nice little nest egg. It's way too soon, however, to be concerned about that.

I really enjoy my work. I'd be lost without it. It's not true that I'm just hanging on here waiting to become eligible for retirement.

I'll worry about all this financial business sometime soon. Right now I've got more important things on my mind.

The more I make, the more I'll be able to save. I'm sure that even though the kids are growing up our expenses won't increase as fast as my earnings.

You just have to be insured for hospitalization, collision, . . . (and everything else that somebody sells a policy to cover).

It's patriotic to buy government bonds. They need the money and besides there's almost no risk.

Kids get more out of college if they have to work to pay their own way.

We have social security and by the time we retire, they'll have raised the benefits enough to take care of all our needs.

There are places in this country where you can retire on almost nothing.

Grandfather worked every day of his life.

We're going to get a little farm and be completely self-sufficient.

I just live from day to day. All the plans you make will only turn out to be useless, because you really can't see what's going to happen. Sufficient unto the day is the evil thereof.

You can't possibly predict what's going to happen ten years from now or even one year from now. What is the point of planning ahead?

Someday our ship will come in.

After the kids leave home and the mortgage is paid off, it will cost us practically nothing to live.

One of these days a really great money-making opportunity will come along. All one has to do is be ready to grab it.

Money is the root of all evil. (Remember the original. It's love of money that causes all the trouble.)

Dad told me all about 1929. You're never going to get me into the stock market.

Our kids are just starting pre-school. College is a very long way off.

One of these days I'm going to get out of the rat race and
move to Alaska,
sell real estate,
raise apples,
devote full time to the stock market,
go into business for myself,
go back to school,
write novels,

. . . .

Well, I think you get the idea. Some of these may seem sort of sacred to you. All I'm suggesting is a good hard look at them and what seems to be behind them. These things seem to me to be frequent deterrents to our efforts to formulate reasonable goals and GRS programs.

9

If You're So Smart, Why Aren't You Rich?

Wrapping it up and trying to answer some of the tough questions which people keep asking.

Giving Advice

The real effectiveness of self-directed change and the importance of working it all out for one's self, poses a real problem for me. If I tell you exactly how I think you should do it, you'll react to the implied criticism, resist as you tend to resist all changes in your behavior instigated by others, and just not be very interested. I can't supply a lot of details about what you should do if there is going to be any long-run change in your financial operations. On the other hand, that's what you've come to expect from books on how to get rich. Whether or not the books have delivered the goods, their publishers are always offering you "clear, step by step instructions on how to achieve instant wealth." All the evidence I've seen which relates to changing behavior, says this is the wrong way to do it. Perhaps the results you've actually observed from these "step by step" books simply adds to this evidence. So don't be disappointed that the kitchen recipes don't appear here. There are some things that you've simply got to work out for yourself. You can't just be told about them if they are going to mean anything in your life. For many of us religion is like this. You've got to do more than read about it. You've got to work out the conclusions for yourself, if they are going to be influential in your conduct. So much about getting interested in a GRS program, working one out, and actually following it through, depends on you. I've been about as specific as I dare to be without getting you hung up on the details of my own ways of doing these things. Grab the concept and work out the details for yourself. It's far more important to do the right things than to do things right, as some contemporary philosopher has announced.

Having said that, I'll go right ahead trying to sell you on some more ideas, by way of kind of pulling things together.

This whole business of goals, track records, and GRS plans may simply seem like far too much trouble to you. Rather than have me try to talk you into it with passionate exhortations, make some experiments, very inexpensive experiments, to find out how much trouble these things really are and how much effort you could comfortably invest in such doings. Don't just dump the whole concept. Try your own simpler, easier version of all this. Invest the little bit of effort just to get these ideas under way. Try as much of this as *doesn't* seem like too much trouble to you. But above all, whatever you do, try something. Be enough of a scientist to give it at least the minimum experimental test. The basic behavioral tenet of those who study themselves is, "How do I know what I think until I see what I do?"

Fringes

If getting rich slowly seems like too much sweat to you, think about some of the side benefits that come free with the tuition.

You are very likely to learn some things about yourself that will make you a better, more effective, more self-respecting person in everything you do, not just in your financial operations.

Making plans and working out skillfully conceived financial operations will get to be a lot of fun. The more effort you put into it and the more experience you get, the more fun it is likely to be. Like most things in life, it doesn't depend for success on deadly seriousness.

This kind of program is going to give you a special sense of satisfaction over the responsible way you've met some of your obligations to your family and to yourself. It's one of the good things you can do for those who are good to you.

The time you spend on your GRS program is time you're not spending watching TV, talking to a bar tender, or thinking about that little cookie you probably ought not to think about.

I've necessarily left the details of how to do it pretty much in your hands. Here's a chance to be imaginative, creative, insightful, and operate at your highest intellectual level. You may find a special fulfillment in working out your GRS program. The satisfaction of watching your net worth grow according to plans of your own careful formulation is immense.

If it turns out that I'm right, that you can do all this by working it out for yourself, that you'll get much better actual results than by reading someone else's rules from a book; if it turns out that way, you'll be pretty pleased with yourself. You may even get sufficiently enthusiastic to want to share the concepts with others and perhaps you'll write a far better book than this.

In Three Lessons

As I see it, there are three basic things to do. This is as close as I want to come to the "ten easy lessons" ploy.

1/ Make your GRQ experiment. Even if you're sure you don't need it, make it.

2/ Put together your goals and the investment media you find most comfortable in a GRS program. Get it written down. Your basic operating rule should be to make decisions so as to maximize the probability of achieving your objectives.

3/ Don't be embarrassed to get really interested in yourself as the subject of some very useful research. Start developing your track record. Take the view that you and the market are parts of an interacting system. See what you can do to discover the useful regularities in your behavior and the predictable ways you are influenced by the market.

If all of this makes even the slightest sense to you, talk it over with your spouse, your kids, or someone who'll listen seriously. Talking about it will do a lot to help you clarify your own beliefs and understand your wants. "How do I know what I think until I hear what I say?" You'll perhaps catch the contagious spark of enthusiasm that you generate in those with whom you talk. To talk with others is to strengthen your own convictions.

Questions

As I've talked to people about these ideas, I've strengthened my convictions, but I've also gotten lots of questions, lots of objections, and, I suspect, lots of resisted urges to label it all baloney. The latter I can't say much about, but the former seem to have consisted mostly of questions like these:

1/ Isn't it true that the only way one can make money in the stock market is to be an insider?

Inside information may be one of the ways to achieve consistently superior performance, but there are lots of ways of achieving average performance at any given level of risk. My notion is simply that if you get in there and achieve average performance, you'll end up a lot better off than the vast majority of people.

2/ Looking at the past performance of a stock, an approach to the market, or an advisory service, really doesn't offer any guarantees about what will happen in the future. How can one be sure?

One can't, of course, be sure. The whole structure of science is built on finding historical regularities in the universe and these regularities are usually imperfect. To study the past is to reduce one's uncertainty about the future, not to become certain of the future. The more dependable a systematic effect appears on the basis of past data, the smaller our uncertainty will be about its future. The key to making sense of this past-future dilemma is to begin to be explicit about your uncertainty. Watch out for those who sound certain of the future. They are usually trying to sell something.

3/ What has all this to do with decision theory, systems analysis, and things like that?

I have tried to spare you the jargon and some of the ponderous expressions favored by those of us who work in these fields. Let me simply say that if you read a contemporary book on decision theory or systems analysis you will, I hope, find the ideas compatible with what you've read here. We have worked with qualitative, non-mathematical versions of some notions which can be dealt with in quite sophisticated symbolic and quantitative forms.

4/ How about this or that mathematical technique?

The techniques mentioned include all sorts of things like portfolio analysis, alpha and beta coefficients, multiple correlation models, factor analysis, industrial dynamics, large scale system simulation models, and so on.

These things are interesting, complex, expensive, and largely beside the point in my opinion. Beside the point, if you agree with me that the real problem in getting rich is to get you and me to do our part, not to develop slightly more subtle understandings of the market itself. My guess is that these techniques are not even close to being cost-effective for us as individuals. Let the big banks and institutions work on them for a while.

5/ Can't you be more specific about what to buy? What do you recommend right now?

I'm flattered to be asked, but "No, I can't be more specific." It depends a lot on you and a little bit on the market and the economy. If you were me and had my GRS plan I'd say, "The next time the market is down, buy an aggressive no-load mutual fund." But you have to know yourself and develop your own GRS plan.

6/ Can you prove that your ideas will work?

I can offer the very same sort of proof that other people who have ideas about accumulating wealth can offer you. If you had done so and so at such and such a time, you would be thus and so wealthy now. In other words, these ideas can be shown to work on the basis of past data. Not only that, but with a far greater degree of reliability than most ideas which involve GRQ opportunities. But this isn't the kind of proof that I'm concerned about. You have to do your part or nothing will work at all. Only you can prove to yourself whether or not you can do what is required to plan and execute a GRQ program. In this very important sense, only you can develop the proof and you need confidence enough in yourself to have a go at it. I'm not trying to be tricky. Just honest enough to be able to sleep with the thought that somebody might just stake his financial future on these notions.

7/ Why are you telling us all this?

It' s fun to help people, and I'm convinced that these ideas can be helpful. As I said in the preface, if you buy the book I'll be pleased because I can use the money. Finally, I'm professionally interested in the practical applications of science and the broader use of engineering concepts. This book is part of an effort in that direction.

8/ If you're so smart, why aren't you rich?

Well, by my criteria I'm getting rich slowly and pretty surely. I've got a GRS program, I'm reviewing it at my annual milestones, and it's working out fairly well. When the market was up at the end of 1968, I felt great about things. All through the bear market which followed I felt kind of frustrated and wondered a lot. Now that the market has recovered to a degree, I feel better again. Through it all I've kept working at my track record, and many of the things I've written about here I've seen in myself. I'm not sure that my progress will help you make your own plans, but if so, you should know that I've become convinced of these ideas by seeing them work out over more than twenty years.

The last thing I want to do is not wish you luck, but wish you a growing skill. The whole idea is to depend as little as possible on luck.

Appendix

Adjusted Gross Income Class	Total Number of Returns	Average Tax Paid	Number Showing No Tax Due
Over $1-million	624	$984,862	3
Over $500,000	2,393	483,089	22
Over $200,000	15,323	177,161	112
Over $100,000	77,899	73,678	394
Over $50,000	429,568	28,886	1,338

UNCERTAINTY EXPRESSION SCALES

Statement Number	Scale 1	Scale 2		Scale 3					Difficulty
1	H M L	VH H M L VL	0	25	50	75	100		E D
2	H M L	VH H M L VL	0	25	50	75	100		E D
3	H M L	VH H M L VL	0	25	50	75	100		E D
4	H M L	VH H M L VL	0	25	50	75	100		E D
5	H M L	VH H M L VL	0	25	50	75	100		E D
6	H M L	VH H M L VL	0	25	50	75	100		E D
7	H M L	VH H M L VL	0	25	50	75	100		E D
8	H M L	VH H M L VL	0	25	50	75	100		E D
9	H M L	VH H M L VL	0	25	50	75	100		E D
10	H M L	VH H M L VL	0	25	50	75	100		E D
11	H M L	VH H M L VL	0	25	50	75	100		E D
12	H M L	VH H M L VL	0	25	50	75	100		E D
13	H M L	VH H M L VL	0	25	50	75	100		E D
14	H M L	VH H M L VL	0	25	50	75	100		E D
15	H M L	VH H M L VL	0	25	50	75	100		E D
16	H M L	VH H M L VL	0	25	50	75	100		E D
17	H M L	VH H M L VL	0	25	50	75	100		E D
18	H M L	VH H M L VL	0	25	50	75	100		E D
19	H M L	VH H M L VL	0	25	50	75	100		E D
20	H M L	VH H M L VL	0	25	50	75	100		E D
21	H M L	VH H M L VL	0	25	50	75	100		E D
22	H M L	VH H M L VL	0	25	50	75	100		E D
23	H M L	VH H M L VL	0	25	50	75	100		E D
24	H M L	VH H M L VL	0	25	50	75	100		E D
25	H M L	VH H M L VL	0	25	50	75	100		E D
26	H M L	VH H M L VL	0	25	50	75	100		E D
27	H M L	VH H M L VL	0	25	50	75	100		E D
28	H M L	VH H M L VL	0	25	50	75	100		E D
29	H M L	VH H M L VL	0	25	50	75	100		E D
30	H M L	VH H M L VL	0	25	50	75	100		E D

Note: Any response that takes less than about ten seconds should be rated easy - E. If it takes more than ten seconds, rate it difficult - D. Look at your watch for ten seconds to get a rough idea how long this is; then simply make some rough judgments about your response times.

SCALE FREQUENCIES AND DIFFICULTY RATINGS

		No Response	Scale 1	Scale 2	Scale 3	E Difficulty	D Difficulty
1.	All Statements						
2.	Direct Experience: 8, 11, 16						
	Cards, Dice, Coins: 6, 7, 28						
	Sports: 1, 5, 21						
	Stock Market: 18, 19, 20						
	The Company: 3, 4, 9						
	Politics: 24, 26, 27						
	The Economy: 13, 23, 25						
	Science and Technology: 12, 14, 15						
	Sampling: 2, 10, 17						
3.	Past Events 11, 17, 18, 22, 27						
	Future Events 1, 4, 5, 8, 12						
4.	Statements 1 - 8						
	Statements 21 - 28						
5.	Five Highest Responses						
	Five Lowest Responses						
	Five Responses Nearest Midpoint						
6.	E Rated Responses						
	D Rated Responses						
7.	Socially Acceptable 2, 6, 7, 10, 19, 28						
	Unusual 3, 8, 11, 14, 16, 22						
8.	Unique Events 1, 5, 8, 22						
	Replicable Events 2, 6, 7, 28						
9.	Additional Information:						
	Five Most Desired:						
	Five Least Desired:						

MULTIPLICATION FACTOR FOR COMPUTING THE
FUTURE VALUE OF AN INVESTMENT

Number of Years	Equivalent Interest Rate				
	5%	10%	15%	20%	25%
5	1.28	1.61	2.01	2.49	3.05
10	1.63	2.59	4.05	6.19	9.31
15	2.08	4.18	8.14	15.41	28.42
20	2.65	6.73	16.37	38.34	86.74
25	3.39	10.83	32.92	95.40	264.70

Example:

The future value of an investment of $5000 after 15 years at an equivalent interest rate of 20% is

($5000)(15.41) = $77,050

MULTIPLICATION FACTOR FOR COMPUTING THE FUTURE
VALUE OF A SERIES OF EQUAL ANNUAL INVESTMENTS

Number of Years	Equivalent Interest Rate					
	5%	10%	15%	20%	25%	
5	5.53	6.10	6.74	7.44	8.21	
10	12.59	15.94	20.30	25.96	33.25	
15	21.60	31.77	47.58	72.03	109.69	
20	33.07	57.27	102.44	186.69	342.94	
25	47.73	98.35	212.79	471.98	1054.79	

Example:

The value of 10 year-end investments of $2000 each at an equivalent interest rate of 20% is

$$(\$2000)(25.96) = \$51,920$$

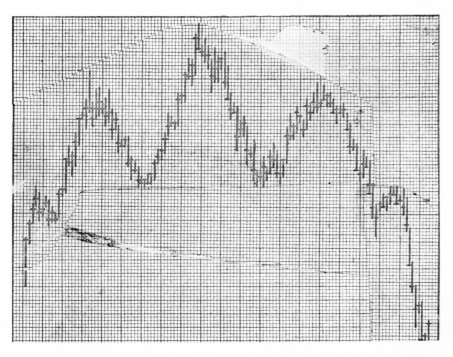

A graph of daily price movements illustrating the "Head and Shoulders Top" formation.

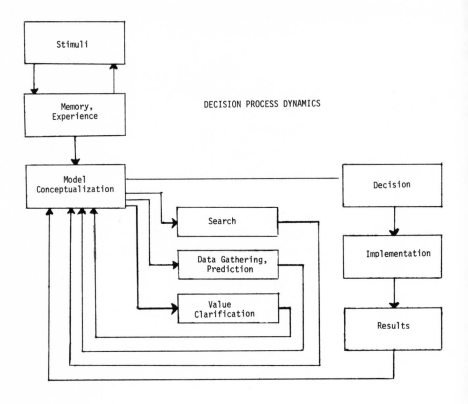

DEVELOPING YOUR STANDARDS OF REASONABLENESS

Consider which of the following statements about decision making you generally agree with, and which you generally disagree with.

On the table which follows, circle the number of each statement with which you generally agree. Count the number of circles in each column of the table and record this number at the bottom of each column.

This data will permit your testing of some of the hypotheses which are suggested. After you have looked over your results, make a first try at formulating some standards of reasonableness for yourself.

1/ The way one makes decisions is not very important. What counts, what one gets paid for is how they turn out. Results are what it's all about.

2/ In making a decision, it is possible to get too much information as well as too little.

3/ One ought to make decisions in such a way as to know pretty clearly what one is doing.

4/ The advice of others should usually be sought in important decisions.

5/ Really good doctors diagnose largely on the basis of intuition. No computer could ever come close to rivalling the performance of an experienced human diagnostician.

6/ Most decisions involve subtle, judgmental, complex considerations which just cannot be written down or talked about. One has to feel them.

7/ Most of the really effective professionals in the stock market rely entirely on intuition.

8/ Deciding among wines, works of art, or books is entirely a matter of taste. Nothing could be done to assist one in making such choices.

9/ One should work at a decision until one gets a strong, clear feeling of the right course of action.

10/ The clearer one is about one's objectives, goals, or targets, the better the decision.

11/ The more objective one can be, the better the decisions he makes.

12/ All decisions involve emotions to some extent and there is no use trying to avoid emotional involvement.

13/ One should never take an action until it is certain that all possible alternatives have been considered.

14/ In making a decision, it is very important to avoid leaving out any consideration or simplifying the situation.

15/ Decisions should not be made hurriedly.

16/ One should be sure to do everything possible to obtain all the relevant information before making a decision.

17/ In making a decision, one cannot go on too long trying to find additional alternative courses of action. There comes a time when it makes sense to choose the best of those one has so far identified.

18/ It usually pays to stop and try to define clearly what one wants to achieve, before making a decision.

19/ The criterion for a good decision is the degree to which one can look back on it without regret, no matter how it turns out.

20/ Good decisions often involve, intuitive, seat-of-the-pants, top-of-the-head methods which cannot really be explained.

21/ Generally speaking one should discuss a decision with somebody else before going ahead.

22/ It is important to be able to explain or justify one's decisions, to one's self as well as to others.

23/ The best way to make a decision is to sort of immerse one's self in the situation until one gets a feel for what should be done.

24/ The more one can write down about a decision, talk about it, explain it, or seek the advice of others, the better the decision.

25/ Decisions which are important should involve some use of paper and pencil to write down the relevant considerations.

26/ The human mind is capable of considering, in ways which we cannot yet explain, a vast array of complex aspects of any decision situation.

27/ Important decisions should be avoided when one is very tired, distracted, or emotionally upset.

28/ As long as there is any possibility of finding a better course of action, one should keep on looking.

29/ To the extent that decisions involve calculations, it is very important to avoid mistakes in arithmetic.

30/ The objective of any decision aiding tool or expert advisor is to guarantee that one makes the right decision.

31/ Really good decision makers are never uncertain about how things will turn out.

32/ It is not unreasonable for people to be able to choose a course of action without being able to say very clearly what their goals or objectives may be.

33/ All decisions involve some degree of risk. What is important is to take sensible, calculated risks.

34/ Uncertainty about the results of one's actions is unavoidable, but it makes sense to do what is necessary to reduce that uncertainty to a reasonable level.

35/ One should always write down, or discuss explicitly the alternative courses of action among which one is choosing.

A	B	C	D	E	F	G	H	I	J
	1								
				2					
			3						
			4						
		5							
		6							
		7							
							8		
						9			
						10			
11									
	12								
								13	
	14								
15									
					16				
									17
						18			
19									
		20							
			21						
			22						
		23							
			24						
			25						
	26								
27									
								28	
29									
	30								
					31				
							32		
			33						
			34						
			35						

Hypotheses About Standards of Reasonableness

1/ The larger the number in column A, the more reasonable are your expectations about the benefits of decision analysis.

2/ The larger the number in column B, the greater the opportunity for further development of your expectations about the benefits of decision analysis.

3/ The larger the number in column C, the greater your tendency toward intuitive, implicit decision making.

4/ The larger the number in column D, the greater your tendency toward explicit, open decision making.

5/ The larger the number in column E, the more reasonable is your approach to uncertainty about future events.

6/ The larger the number in column F, the greater the opportunity for further development of your approach toward uncertainty about future events.

7/ The larger the number in column G, the greater your tendency to be clear and explicit about your goals.

8/ The larger the number in column H, the greater the opportunity for further clarification of your goals.

9/ The larger the number in column I, the greater your tendency to persist in search for better courses of action.

Formulate three rough standards of reasonableness by which you would be willing to judge the quality of your own decisions.

1.

2.

3.

Some Suggestions for Further Reading

Loeb, Gerald M., *The Battle for Investment Survival.* New York. Simon and Schuster. 1965 (one of the great classics)

Brealey, Richard A., *An Introduction to Risk and Return from Common Stocks.* Cambridge. The MIT Press, 1969 (an outstanding introduction to the random walk hypothesis and contemporary research)

Edwards, Robert D., and John Magee, *Technical Analysis of Stock Trends.* Springfield, John Magee. 1966 (the basic bible of technical analysis)

Livermore, Jesse L., *How to Trade in Stocks.* Palisades Park, N.J., The Investor's Press. 1940 (a grand old example of a GRQ program)

Horney, Karen, *Self-Analysis.* New York, W. W. Norton, 1942 (looking at yourself with the help of a Psychiatrist)

Engel, Louis, *How to Buy Stocks.* New York, Bantam Books, 1962 (one of the best sources of the basic knowledge needed to begin)

Your Attitude Toward Risk

One way to get an impression of your attitudes toward risk is to plot your utility function for money.

On the next page are twelve decisions, each of which has a 50/50 gamble as one alternative and a sure dollar income or outflow, called a sum certain, as the other alternative. You should fill in the blanks with sums of money which would make you indifferent between the two alternatives.

In Decision 1 you have a choice between

a fifty percent chance of $100 and a fifty percent chance of nothing

A dollars for sure

For what value of *A* would you be indifferent? What amount of money would be just as attractive to you as flipping a coin for $100 or nothing?

Fill in your indifference value of *A*. Enter the same value in the *A* blank in Decisions 3, 4, 6, and 13.

Continue in the same way until all the blanks are filled.

Turn to the utility function graph. Plot your *A* value on the horizontal line marked *A*. Continue in this way, plotting your *E* value on the line labelled *E*, and so on.

Starting at the point already appearing in the upper right, connect your plotted values with a line passing through the origin. You now have a first cut at your utility function.

If the curve tends to "flop over" increasing less steeply as it goes up, you are "risk averse." You tend to avoid taking risks unless there is a big potential payoff. You are likely to be well insured, hold a diversified portfolio of stocks, avoid commercial gambling, and generally exhibit caution about taking chances with your money.

If the curve tends to point upward, increasing more steeply as it rises, you are a risk taker. You are likely to be insured only against major risks, hold one or a small number of highly speculative stocks, enjoy gambling, and generally exhibit a willingness to take chances with your money in the hope of large profits.

Utility Scaling Work Sheet

A 50/50 chance of either   Sum certain

1. $100 or nothing   A = _____
2. E = _____ or $100   nothing
3. A = _____ or $100   K = _____
4. A = _____ or nothing   B = _____
5. E = _____ or nothing   F = _____
6. A = _____ or B = _____   L = _____
7. E = _____ or F = _____   M = _____
8. B = _____ or nothing   C = _____
9. F = _____ or nothing   G = _____
10. F = _____ or G = _____   N = _____
11. G = _____ or nothing   H = _____
12. $100 or K = _____   D = _____
13. K = _____ or A = _____   J = _____

UTILITY FUNCTION GRAPH

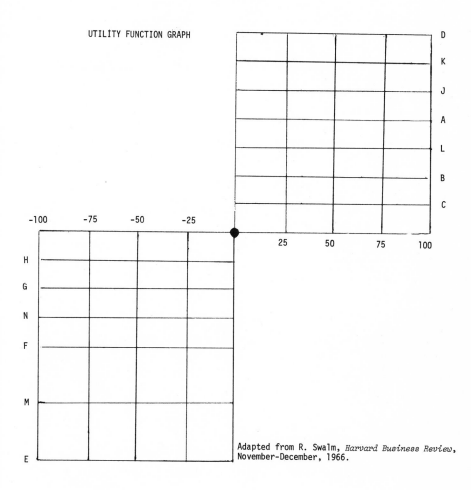

Adapted from R. Swalm, *Harvard Business Review*,
November-December, 1966.

Index